SEX MAGICK

NICHOLAS BROWN

CURRENT THEATRE SERIES

First published in 2023
by Currency Press Pty Ltd,
PO Box 2287, Strawberry Hills, NSW, 2012, Australia
enquiries@currency.com.au
www.currency.com.au

in association with Griffin Theatre Company

Copyright: *Sex Magick* © Nicholas Brown, 2023.

COPYING FOR EDUCATIONAL PURPOSES

The Australian *Copyright Act 1968* [Act] allows a maximum of one chapter or 10% of this book, whichever is the greater, to be copied by any educational institution for its educational purposes provided that that educational institution [or the body that administers it] has given a remuneration notice to Copyright Agency [CA] under the Act.

For details of the CA licence for educational institutions contact CA, 12/66 Goulburn Street, Sydney, NSW, 2000; tel: within Australia 1800 066 844 toll free; outside Australia 61 2 9394 7600; fax: 61 2 9394 7601; email: memberservices@copyright.com.au

COPYING FOR OTHER PURPOSES

Except as permitted under the Act, for example a fair dealing for the purposes of study, research, criticism or review, no part of this book may be reproduced, stored in a retrieval system, or transmitted in any form or by any means without prior written permission. All enquiries should be made to the publisher at the address above.

Any performance or public reading of *Sex Magick* is forbidden unless a licence has been received from the author or the author's agent. The purchase of this book in no way gives the purchaser the right to perform the play in public, whether by means of a staged production or a reading. All applications for public performance should be addressed to the author c/- Currency Press at the address above.

Typeset by Brighton Gray for Currency Press.
Printed by Fineline Print + Copy Services, Revesby, NSW.
Cover features Raj Labade. Photo by Brett Boardman, design by Alphabet.

 A catalogue record for this book is available from the National Library of Australia

Contents

SEX MAGICK 1

Theatre Program at the end of the playtext

Sex Magick was first produced by Griffin Theatre Company in association with Sydney WorldPride 2023 at The Stables Theatre, Darlinghurst, on 17 February, 2023, with the following cast:

ARD / YOUNG KEERAN	Raj Labade
CINDY / GONDESHWAR / ALLI-JANE / MISC.	Blazey Best
LIRAZ / YOUNG CINDY / JOJO / MISC.	Catherine Văn-Davies
BOYD / YOUNG ANAND / COREY / MISC.	Mansoor Noor
MANMATHA / DRAYTON / GAZZA / MISC.	Stephen Madsen
KEERAN / ARDH-ANARISH-VARA / ANAND / WAYLON / MISC.	Veshnu Narayanasamy

Playwright & Co-Director, Nicholas Brown
Dramaturg & Co-Director, Declan Greene
Choreographer, Raghav Handa
Set & Costume Designer, Mason Browne
Lighting Designer, Kelsey Lee
Composer & Sound Designer, Danni A. Esposito
Video Designer, Solomon Thomas
Associate Cultural Dramaturg, Jay Emmanuel
Community Engagement Director, Gary Paramanathan
Creative Producer Bali Padda
Intimacy Coordinator, Chloe Dallimore
Malayalam Translation, Anish Chacko, Athira Pradeep, Rashmi Ravindran
Stage Manager, Isabella Kerdijk

ACKNOWLEDGEMENTS

For support of the script development of *Sex Magick*, thanks to Playwriting Australia and Australian Plays Transform, Playking Foundation, and the Malcolm Robertson Foundation.

Special thanks also to Daniel Clarke, Ben Graetz, and Lisa Freshwater at Sydney WorldPride, Joanne Kee and National Theatre of Paramatta, Belvoir, Nathan Mayfield, Imogen Gardam, Arjunan Puveendran, Matt Mostyn, Raina Peterson, Imara Savage, Leila Enright, Christie Evangelisto, Tim Roseman, Michelle Kotevski, Jay Emmanuel, Romy Bartz, Diana McClean and Gavin Walburgh.

CHARACTERS

ARD PANICKER, a half-Indian, half-Australian man, 30. A sports physiotherapist.

CINDY PANICKER, Ard's mother. A Caucasian woman in her 50s. Vice-chairman of the Hyperions Rugby League Club.

LIRAZ, a businesswoman in her early 30s who runs Shakthi Health Spa.

MANMATHA, a tantric guru, 30s. Any ethnicity but South Asian.

BOYD, a nurse/carer in his early 30s. South Asian-Australian man.

KEERAN, Ard's father. A South Asian man in his late 50s/60s.

YOUNG MAN, a young Indian Kathakali dancer from Kerala.

GONDESHWAR, an Eastern European ashram devotee.

ALLI-JANE, an Australian businesswoman.

WINSOME, a queer member of the Body Somatic.

JOJO, a stripper.

YOUNG WOMAN, an Australian woman in Kerala.

DRAYTON, a publicist.

GAZZA, a Rugby League player.

DOCTOR LES, a doctor at St Vincent's Hospital.

NURSE NICK, a nurse.

COREY, a South Asian American ashram devotee.

YOUNG ANAND, a young Kathakali dancer from Kerala.

WAYLON, Cindy's fiancé.

ARDHA-ANARISH-VARA, an Indian deity.

ANAND, a Kathakali dancer from Kerala.

There is also a voiceover or FaceTime video footage required of a phone conversation with TJ, a trans man in his 30s.

This play text went to press before the end of rehearsals and may differ from the play as performed.

ACT ONE

SCENE ONE

The Indian deity ARDHA-NARISH-VARA *appears, dressed in a splendid, ornate Kathakali outfit—adorned with necklaces, bracelets, bangles, and bells.*

The right-hand side of the outfit is representative of Goddess Shakthi, the left-hand side represents Lord Shiva.

On their head is an enormous headdress, split through with a long, sharp rod.

Red light fills the stage for a moment as their face twitches and contorts into the Kathakali facial expression of Karunam.

ARDHA-NARISH-VARA: Rasa One: Karunam. Suffering.

CINDY PANICKER, *a Caucasian woman in her late 50s, walks to her front door. She's dressed in a power suit. She opens the door to find her son* ARD (*a half South Indian / half Australian man*). *He has a large backpack with him and is extremely sweaty and dishevelled. He bursts through the door.*

CINDY: Ard. What are you doing here?

ARD: Mum.

ARD *falls to his mother's feet in a heap, crying.*

CINDY: Get up. Don't cry on my shoes. They're suede. I haven't Scotchgarded them yet. What's happened to you? There are photographers everywhere. Come inside.

CINDY *leads* ARD *inside. He sees several bronze statues of male Rugby League players looking like ancient Greek gods. A large office chair is close by. On the other side of the stage is a large closet.*

ARD: What have you done?

CINDY: Just a few renovations. Like my new plaque? Cindy Panicker—co-chairman of the Hyperions.

ARD: Where are the walls?
CINDY: I want expansiveness.
ARD: Is that a statue of Kollam?
CINDY: It's a bronze tribute to your brother—yes. Donated by the prime minister. You look awful darling. What happened while you were gone? I'm all ears.

A car horn beeps.

Shit. That's my ride.

CINDY runs to the door.

ARD: Where are you going?
CINDY: Waylon's … Waylon and I are … going to a party.
ARD: Whose party?
CINDY: I … I didn't expect you'd be back this week, Ard. And I didn't want to tell you like this but … here we are. It's my engagement party. Waylon and I are getting married.

ARD suddenly gasps as his face starts twitching. He starts to lose control of his facial muscles.

CINDY: What are you doing?
ARD: I can't control it.

ARD sits in the nearby office chair, holds his stomach and shits himself.

CINDY: My ergonomic chair! /
ARD: Aaaargh.
CINDY: / I just had it ergonomically assessed!
ARD: Help me.
CINDY: Get up and go to the bathroom.
ARD: I can't.
CINDY: Go and have a shower. Take the elevator to level two.
ARD: There's an elevator?

CINDY points to the closet.

CINDY: That's my new voice-activated towel cupboard. Grab yourself a towel. The password's kollam.
ARD: Keep talking to me, Mum. I don't wanna pass out.

The horn beeps again outside.

CINDY: Ahhh. We're having the wedding in the stadium. Will you walk me down the field?
ARD: Doesn't Waylon wanna have the wedding in a church?
CINDY: The footy field is our church. We're borrowing the decorations from Hillsong.
ARD: But you're an atheist.
CINDY: I like Christmas and crucifixes. Do you need some water?
ARD: Just keep talking to me.
CINDY: Ahhh. I've been doing Christian cross-fit classes at Waylon's gym. It's called Cruci-fit.
ARD: I can't feel my face.

Cindy's phone rings. It's a 'Simply the Best' by Tina Turner/ Rugby League ringtone. She answers it.

CINDY: Waylon. Shit. My battery's just about to run out. I can't come to the party. Because Ard's come home and he's acting really strange.
ARD: Mum—go.
CINDY: I can't come, Waylon. I'm sorry.
ARD: You can't not go to your own engagement party.
CINDY: I don't care, Waylon. Just apologise and say I couldn't make it—

The phone conks out.

ARD: It's in my feet Mum. It's in my hands now.
CINDY: Have you been scratched by a bat?
ARD: Aaaaargh!

ARD's fit moves to his whole body. He stands up and thrashes around the room.

CINDY: I'll call an ambulance.

CINDY exits. The fit soon subsides. ARD stands up, rattled and afraid. A rattling noise is heard from the closet. ARD moves to it and tries to open it. Suddenly ARDHA-NARISH-VARA crashes out of the closet in a blaze of drums and cymbals.

SCENE TWO

The deafening sound of cicadas and jungle birds. Swatting away mosquitos and covered in sweat, ARD *and* LIRAZ *appear, trudging with huge backpacks.* LIRAZ *carries a crumpled and ripped paper map.* ARD *throws his backpack on the ground.*

ARD: I can't walk anymore!
LIRAZ: Get up. We're nearly there. I think.
ARD: Traffic's insane here.

We hear a loud rikshaw horn.

LIRAZ: Those rikshaw horns are loud. They startle me.
ARD: My horn startles you.
LIRAZ: Ard.
ARD: Where's the resort? I need to taste you. Now.
LIRAZ: Mile-high sex not enough for you?
ARD: So hot. But I want more.
LIRAZ: Let's just check into the luxury huts first.
ARD: Looks dodgy round here. This is like the beginning of one of those horror movies when the honeymooners arrive at a ranch.
LIRAZ: Honeymooners?
ARD: They always hook up and get nude before the baddy comes to get 'em.
LIRAZ: Can you help me with this map? The fax said to walk through the forest to the beach.
ARD: Who faxes anymore?
LIRAZ: Oh! Look at the peacocks!
ARD: They look pretty skanky to me. I bet the resort put them here.
LIRAZ: No. They're wild peacocks. We're in India Ard. The real India. Authentic to the core.

    GONDESHWAR *enters. She is a Caucasian woman of Eastern European descent, in her 50s. She's dressed in South Indian attire and is holding a hessian bag.*

GONDESHWAR: Namaste! Namaskaar! Welcome! I am Gondeshwar. Right hand of Guru-ji. You must be Liraz D'mour?

ACT ONE

LIRAZ: Yes I'm Liraz.
GONDESHWAR: This must your husband be, Ard Panicker?
ARD: Yes—I'm Liraz's husband.
GONDESHWAR: Good. I made clear in fax that couples doing this course be married must be.

    COREY, *a South Asian American man runs onstage, covered in sweat and struggling for breath. He speaks with an American accent.*

COREY: Gondeshwar! Gondeshwar!
GONDESHWAR: Corey! Do you have enrolment papers?
COREY: Guru-ji's furious that two students have missed the induction initiation.
GONDESHWAR: It not is my fault. You in charge of administration Corey! Is he really furious? Or just little bit cross again?
COREY: He's really mad Gondeshwar. He's got that look in his eye.
GONDESHWAR: I hope he does not beat us again.
COREY: Are these the late comers? Guru-ji's waiting. You both need to move into the amphitheatre immediately.
GONDESHWAR: You may call him Guru-ji or Manmatha-ji. Always say ji after saying his name for respect. And if he put his foot near your face, kiss it.
COREY: Wait. They don't have their tilaks.
GONDESHWAR: I was about to just do it Corey.
COREY: But Guru-ji asked me to—
GONDESHWAR: Corey. Don't rain on my grenade.
COREY: I think you actually mean—
GONDESHWAR: Go!

    COREY *exits.*

Don't mind Corey. He very new here. Only been here ten years and want to be Guru-ji's right hand. Corey's right hand only good for washing my ass. This is your tilak. It help you open up your chakras.

    GONDESHWAR *pulls out a small bottle of red dye from her bag and marks* LIRAZ *on her forehead.*

LIRAZ: Mmmm. Thank you Gondeshwar-ji. Should I wear a scarf around my head too?

GONDESHWAR: Whatever. Just make sure you have loose pants on. Panicker. Your turn.
ARD: Gondeshwar-ji—which chakra will it open up?
GONDESHWAR: Most say third eye but I say base chakra.
ARD: [*joking to* LIRAZ] That's the one between my balls and a-hole hey?

> LIRAZ *is embarrassed.* GONDESHWAR *marks* ARD*'s forehead—unimpressed.*

GONDESHWAR: Smartie-ass jock huh? I must also collect your phones. It is part of process here. No phones. Put phones in itchy sack.

> ARD *takes his phone out of his pocket and puts it in Gondeshwar's hessian bag.*

LIRAZ: I expected just this and I didn't bring a phone.
GONDESHWAR: You good girl. Nice girl. Pretty girl. You wasting your time with shitty jockstrap here. Come.

> *The world shifts, and we are now in an amphitheatre—with* ARD *and* LIRAZ *seated.* MANMATHA *is onstage, smiling patiently. He is an unassuming, handsome white man.*

MANMATHA: One month with me and you will be gurus yourself. And that concludes the initiation ceremony. Namaste. Welcome to my latecomers. We will all be latecomers shortly and you'll understand what I mean in a moment. We shall meet here for meditation every night after our evening classes, which will be held in the huts just over yonder way.

> ARD *whispers to* LIRAZ.

ARD: Liraz? Why's he teaching this course?
LIRAZ: He seems lovely.
ARD: But he's not Indian. I thought you wanted authentic.
LIRAZ: He could be from Kashmir. They're very fair in the north.
MANMATHA: Do not be late to any of my classes. Broth will be served for breakfast. Plain rice for lunch and salt-free dahl for supper.

> ARD *whispers to* LIRAZ.

ARD: This guy's a fake.

> MANMATHA *moves to* ARD.

MANMATHA: What did you say?
ARD: I said … I feel awake.
LIRAZ: He's woke Guru-ji. So am I.
MANMATHA: [*to* LIRAZ] Yes you are. Welcome back to India, my dear.
LIRAZ: Actually Guru-ji—it's / my first time here.
MANMATHA: You've had many past lives here. Your aura is purple. That means that you're a seeker of truth. You're independent, intellectual, extroverted and authoritative. Oooh those violet rays are illuminating this amphitheatre. I've been double-taking like a slapstick fop on a British stage. Triple-taking in fact. And yes—I can see all of your auras. But that's not why we're here. We are here for sexual awakening. For explosions. Inner explosions. For woman and man—for two forces at opposite poles to come together. This is tantra.
ARD: Tantra?
MANMATHA: And this is why it's paramount that you're in pairs.
ARD: As in tantric sex? I thought this was an aravedic course?
MANMATHA: And that there are even numbers …
LIRAZ: It's pronounced ayurvedic.
MANMATHA: … and no odd ones.

> *Pause.*

> Tantra is the main component of the course. Now this is of utmost importance: couples will be sleeping in separate quarters and you must not have sex for the month you are here.

> ARD *stands and goes to leave.*

> No intercourse, no masturbating, no ejaculating, no orgasms. For a month. Then and only then can you be latecomers. If you break this rule you will be expelled from the course and you will not receive your certificates. Do we all agree? You may clap if the answer is yes.

> LIRAZ *claps. Hopefully the audience all clap too.* ARD *doesn't clap.* MANMATHA *moves to him.*

> Panicker. I can see your aura.
LIRAZ: What colour is it?
MANMATHA: Black.
ARD: What does that mean?

MANMATHA: Death. Your father has died recently.
ARD: How could you know that?
MANMATHA: I can see it in your eyes.

ARD is in disbelief.

Who else would like their aura read?

SCENE THREE

Night. ARD *slams the door of a run-down hut in disgust.* LIRAZ *enters.*

LIRAZ: You okay?
ARD: There was just a masturbating monkey at my door.
LIRAZ: Makes sense right? We learn about the monkey god and then a monkey serenades you at your door.
ARD: I wanna serenade you.
LIRAZ: We're not allowed.
ARD: No-one's sticking to the rules. The woman who served me lentils stuck her finger into my belly button. Let's just fuck in the forest.
LIRAZ: Manmathaj-ji said that it's paramount / for us not to—
ARD: / You're completely in awe of Fuck Fragrance aren't you?
LIRAZ: How could you not be? He's the best looking guru I've ever met.
ARD: Are you into him?
LIRAZ: You jealous?
ARD: No.
LIRAZ: Fuck fragrance?
ARD: I checked Corey's phrase book. Manmatha means sex. And his last name Khushboo means scent. His name means Fuck Fragrance!
LIRAZ: Ard.
ARD: Can we just go back to Sydney and forget about Fuck Fragrance? Please?
LIRAZ: Absolutely not. We're staying here.
ARD: You said we'd be eating off banana leaves and drinking cocktails from coconuts Liraz. Instead we're sleeping in separate huts and we're not allowed to touch each other. Why didn't you tell me this was a tantric course?
LIRAZ: I forgot. Sorry.

ARD: Is there something—should I be doing something differently—am I pleasing you?

GONDESHWAR *enters.*

GONDESHWAR: You should not be in here with door closed.

LIRAZ: Sorry Gondeshwar-ji. I don't want any of those wild peacocks as surprise guests. And the mosquitos were coming in so I closed it.

GONDESHWAR: Come Liraz. Let's go for swim. I want to tell you about the myth of Lord Indra.

GONDESHWAR *begins to lead* LIRAZ *out of the hut as* COREY *enters.*

One hot sunny day (much like this one) the mischievous Lord Indra (who was hot for the wife of a great sage) took on the form of the great sage and made sweet, sweaty love to this wife. But when great sage found out about naughty rumpy pumpy—he curse Lord Indra for his obsession with vagine—and Lord Indra was covered in thousands of vagine—all over his body that later transformed into weeping and seeping eyes.

GONDESHWAR *and* LIRAZ *exit.* COREY *gives* ARD *a pile of books.*

COREY: Study and buddy time.

ARD *groans.*

How're you going with your reading?

ARD: I dunno. There are too many gods. I can't keep track of who's who and what's what. Can't tell if the god in one part of the story is the same in another part. Everyone's an avatar of everyone else. No-one's just themselves. It's all really confusing.

COREY: Welcome to India my friend. Everything seems contradictory on the surface but if you look deeper, honestly, you'll learn the most incredible things about humanity and about yourself.

ARD: I've learnt that lentils look like chunder.

COREY: They're actually an aphrodisiac.

ARD: What's the fricken' point of that when you can't fuck? Nothing makes sense here—mostly Manmatha—he talks a whole lotta shit! And Liraz is lapping it up.

COREY: I can tell you love your wife very much. It must be hard not being able to make love to each other.

ARD: It's driving me mad! But we snuck in a kiss down at the markets—the cops told us off though.
COREY: The moral police. They're all over India.
ARD: It was just a little peck on the lips. I may have grabbed her arse too.
COREY: Sex is sacred in India. It's not something that's flaunted.
ARD: Then how the hell is a dodgy guru teaching tantra?!
COREY: We should read.
ARD: Cos he's white, ay? And white people can do what they want.

*Elsewhere—with the sound of waves crashing on a nearby beach—*LIRAZ *is covertly talking into an iPhone.* ALLI-JANE *appears on the other side of the stage on her phone.*

LIRAZ: Can you hear me now? Hello? Alli-Jane?
ALLI-JANE: Where the fuck are you?
LIRAZ: I can't hear you properly. Can you say that again?
ALLI-JANE: Are you at the beach? Are you on fucking holiday?
LIRAZ: It's a business trip.
ALLI-JANE: A business trip? When your business is falling apart?
LIRAZ: I'm on the trip to try and save the business!
ALLI-JANE: What am I meant to do? The practitioners are all freaking out. Clients are angry, Liraz.
LIRAZ: I'll be back in three weeks.
ALLI-JANE: Three weeks?!
LIRAZ: I swear I'll sort it all out when I'm back.
ALLI-JANE: Where are you? On the Gold Coast?
LIRAZ: Ah. I'm on a coast.
ALLI-JANE: Are you at the Boho Luxe Market at the Psychic and Well Being Exhibition in Brisbane?
LIRAZ: I'm—I'm in Indi— oh—you're breaking up Alli-Jane. I can't hear you.
ALLI-JANE: Are you in India?
LIRAZ: Yes. Yes. I am.
ALLI-JANE: With who?
LIRAZ: A potential masseur. An Indian masseur.
ALLI-JANE: What's her name?

MANMATHA *enters with Gondeshwar's hessian bag.*

LIRAZ: Ard. Panicker.

ALLI-JANE: Panicker. As in Kollam Panicker?
LIRAZ: Yes, as a matter of fact I'm in Kerala with Kollam Panicker's brother.
ALLI-JANE: Why would you be in India with that neanderthal boofhead's brother?!

MANMATHA *signals to* LIRAZ *to hand the phone over.*

LIRAZ: [*pretending to talk to someone else on the phone*] And then the thousands of vaginas that were all over his body transformed into eyes. And they wept and cried as punishment. It's my favourite myth. You'd love it here ... Grandma.
MANMATHA: Give me the phone, Liraz.
ALLI-JANE: Grandma? Who're you talking to you?
MANMATHA: What's the correct thing to do, Liraz?
LIRAZ: Put it in your itchy sack?

LIRAZ *turns off her phone.* ALLI-JANE *exits.* LIRAZ *gives the phone to* MANMATHA. *He takes it but then slowly hands it back to her. He puts his finger up against his lips and then on hers. They smile at each other and exit.*

We return to the hut with COREY *and* ARD.

ARD: Corey, dudes in the street hold hands here. Have you noticed that?
COREY: I have. I think it's sweet. They hold pinky fingers.
ARD: Liraz thinks it's camaraderie.
COREY: What do *you* think it is?
ARD: I dunno.

Pause.

I wanna go home. Don't you ever wanna go home Corey?
COREY: This is home. My parents kicked me out when I was a teenager. Luckily the local Hare Krishna kitchen gave out free meals once a week and I met some beautiful people there. Before I knew it I was living in an ashram in Santa Barbara and then I decided to take it one step further and move here. Haven't looked back. Next year I'll be given a new name. I know Manmatha's provocative and unconventional and I know you doubt him because he's white but ... he's more Indian than I'll ever be. Trust me, he's a healer and he's transformed thousands of lives here. Come here. Stand next to me.

ARD *reluctantly gets up and stands next to* COREY. COREY *slowly wraps his pinky finger around* ARD*'s. They both breathe in deeply.* COREY *smiles at* ARD. ARD *smiles back.*

ARD: Corey, can you keep a secret?
COREY: Of course.
ARD: Liraz isn't my wife. We only met a week ago.

Reality bends around this moment and the sound of screaming cicadas becomes absorbed into the tinny drone of a 'jungle' meditation soundscape—with panpipes, synth, and trickling water. Somewhere nearby, the sound of a cars on a busy street.

SCENE FOUR

LIRAZ *stands with an iPad, looking agitated—stabbing at the screen with her finger. She wears expensive activewear paired with South-Asian-looking beads and bracelets.* ARD *appears in crisp, pressed pants and a polo shirt.*

LIRAZ: Ard Panicker? Yay. You're here. Nice shirt! I'm Liraz. The proprietor of Shakthi Spa. I'm so happy you're here (even though you're late and my schedule's out of whack) but that's okay—I'm calm and present and I'm excited to meet you.
ARD: This place looks rad. A health spa's right up my alley.
LIRAZ: Well—I think you could be right up our alley. You have a very impressive resume. Do you want some wheat grass juice or some champagne?
ARD: Nah. I'm good.
LIRAZ: Yes you are. Well, I'll start by asking a few basic questions about your approach to body work. What colour's my aura?
ARD: I'm sorry?
LIRAZ: My aura? What colour is it?
ARD: Oh. Ah … pink?
LIRAZ: No. It's purple. But that's okay. There's a lot of cosmic radiation in Bondi today. What chakras do you work from when massaging?
ARD: Oh. Ah—my hand sharkras?
LIRAZ: You don't know what chakras are, do you?

ARD *shakes his head.*

They're energy centres on your body. Spinning wheels of energy. Chakra one: the red root chakra—it's between your testicles and your anus.

    ARD *giggles.*

ARD: Sorry.

LIRAZ: Chakra two: orange—where we learn to trust ourselves and others. Chakra three: yellow. Where we hold our self esteem and dealings with fear. Can I touch you?

ARD: Go on.

    She puts her hand on his heart.

LIRAZ: Chakra four: green. The heart. Chakra five: blue. Through its power we speak the truth.

    She puts her hand on his throat.

Chakra six, your third eye: purple—where we hold our psychic power.

    She touches his third eye area.

Chakra seven: white. Your true purpose. The connection to the divine. Come with me.

    We are now in a room of shimmering, reflected light.

This is the water room. We offer spa therapy and treatment involving the application of ice.

    We are now in a room that is dark, shadowy, and enveloping.

This is the earth room. Here you can have a mud bath or a mud wrap.

    We are now in a room that glows with red-hot heat.

This is the fire room, where we offer moxa and Tibetan fire therapy.

ARD: Are you Tibetan?

LIRAZ: No. Are you?

ARD: No.

    We are now in a room that glows with pure white light. ARD *is wearing an oxygen mask.*

LIRAZ: This is the air room where we have aromatherapy in our oxygen bar. Instead of ordering a beer, you order some oxygen.

ARD: Reminds me of when I had my stomach pumped after my cousin's bucks night.

    LIRAZ *is unamused.* ARD *sheepishly removes the oxygen mask.*

LIRAZ: Can you give ayurvedic massages?

ARD: Ahh—yeah—I can give it a crack?

LIRAZ: Do you even …? Your father's from Kerala and you don't know what ayurveda is?

ARD: How'd you know he was from Kerala?

LIRAZ: Panicker. South Indian last name.

ARD: Very good.

LIRAZ: I was Indian in a past life.

ARD: Aha.

LIRAZ: You speak Hindi, don't you? Or Malayalam?

ARD: Nah.

    LIRAZ *is disappointed.* ALLI-JANE *enters.*

ALLI-JANE: A thank you would have been nice.

LIRAZ: For what?

ALLI-JANE: For scrubbing the graffiti from the—

LIRAZ: Ah yes. Thank you Alli-Jane. This is Ard—a prospective practitioner. He was just telling me about how committed he is to hinduism.

    ARD *smiles at* ALLI-JANE.

ALLI-JANE: I see. As you were.

    ALLI-JANE *exits.*

ARD: [*grins*] So, when do I start?

LIRAZ: I'll be in touch after meeting the other applicants.

    LIRAZ *goes to leave.*

ARD: Wait, wait, wait. Okay, I don't know about … like … aru-veda /

LIRAZ: / Ayurveda.

ARD: / or sharkras /

LIRAZ: / Chakras.

ARD: — / or whatever, but I'm the best physiotherapist in Sydney. You saw my CV? I worked for the Hyperions Rugby League team for like ten years.

LIRAZ: Yeah. I saw. Why did they fire you?

ARD: Pardon?

LIRAZ: You don't have a reference from them. I checked—you're not a registered physio anymore—you're license was taken away. What happened?

ARD: We didn't part on good terms. It was time to move on. I needed to grow as a ... therapist. They wanted to hold me back. So how about I give you a trial massage?

LIRAZ: That won't be necessary.

ARD: Your neck's extremely tense. Your shoulders are out of whack—the left one is a lot lower than the right and they look pretty slouched. I'd say you have thoracic kyphosis because of the hyperextension of your upper cervical vertebrae. Sure you don't want me to give you a trial massage?

LIRAZ strips down to her bra and underwear. We are now back in the earth room—dark, pulsating and enveloping.

Ready?

LIRAZ nods and lies back down. ARD begins to give her a strong, deep tissue massage. As the massage progresses, LIRAZ begins to moan involuntarily. There is the sound of cymbals and drums, and cicadas. The massage table and the earth room drop away, as does ARD.

LIRAZ finds herself alone, in a forest—trembling with pleasure. She looks out, and sees something we cannot. The sight of it takes her breath away—and the cymbals and drums rise in intensity, driving towards a shattering climax as LIRAZ writhes on the massage table, moaning loudly in the grip of a powerful orgasm.

ARDHA-NARISH-VARA enters with orange light on them. They move their face into the Kathakali dance facial expression of Adbutham.

ARDHA-NARISH-VARA: Rasa Two: Adbutham. Wonder.

ARDHA-NARISH-VARA exits.

LIRAZ is now back on the table—she pulls herself together and finds ARD confused and backing away.

LIRAZ: Oh my god. What just happened?

They both suddenly run to each other and kiss.

SCENE FIVE

ARD *is standing alone looking up at a huge statue.* MANMATHA *and* LIRAZ *enter eating jalebis (fried Indian sweets).*

MANMATHA: I agree Liraz, the circular swirl of the jalebi reminds me of the spinning wheels of energy in each chakra. These jalebis are infused with ayurvedic herbs too.
LIRAZ: [*giggling*] Really?
MANMATHA: We bought you some jalebi too, Ard.
ARD: Aren't sweets forbidden?
MANMATHA: Don't tell the others.

We hear some dogs barking. LIRAZ *sees them in the distance.*

LIRAZ: Aww. Look at the dogs. They look like dingoes. So cute. Helloooooo babies.

She exits.

MANMATHA: Do you like the mermaid statue?
ARD: My neck's sore from looking up at it.
MANMATHA: Sit down. I'll fix your neck.
ARD: I don't wanna get sand in my undies.

MANMATHA *takes his shirt off and lays it on the sand for* ARD.

MANMATHA: Sit.
ARD: I'm okay. Really. Thank you though. I'm usually the one giving and not receiving. Massages.

MANMATHA *sits on his shirt.*

MANMATHA: You're a giver.
ARD: Wish I'd brought my footy with me. We could have played touch footy with the others.
MANMATHA: I prefer tackle.

ARD *moves further away.*

ARD: Is it safe for Liraz to be playing with the stray dogs?
MANMATHA: They're very friendly.
ARD: They do look like dingoes.

MANMATHA: They could well be dingoes. Lots of Aussie flora and fauna in India surprisingly. There are Australian eucalyptus trees growing in the Nilgiris jungle. Deeply rooted.

MANMATHA *smiles.*

Have you seen the men in lungis painting each other's faces?

ARD: Yeah. What about 'em?

MANMATHA: They're from the local Kathakali dance theatre company. Incredible, epic storytellers they are. And fitter than any athlete or football player. They tell their stories through their eyes. May I look into yours?

ARD: 'Spose.

MANMATHA *looks into* ARD'*s eyes.*

MANMATHA: Your ancestors have lived here for generations, Ard. How did you lose your father?

ARD: I don't wanna talk about my dad.

MANMATHA: Very well. I was an ashram baby. Lived in a commune until I grew hairs under my arms and until my foreskin started moving back naturally. My dad always said that we'd return to Marton once I hit puberty—Marton's in Yorkshire—birthplace of Captain Cook. But I wanted to stay. My great-great-grandfather worked for the East India Company many years ago. It's in my spiritual DNA this country. There's an ancient magick that India possesses—you can deny yourself access or not. I choose not to deny.

ARD: Yeah—well—my dad abandoned us. Married my mum for a visa and then fucked off as soon as he became a citizen. Total prick. No wonder I'm so useless in relationships.

MANMATHA: In what way are you useless?

ARD: I get jealous.

MANMATHA: A deadly sin.

ARD: And I get serious too quickly. My last girlfriend, before Liraz … We'd been seeing each other for like two weeks and I proposed.

MANMATHA: [*laughing*] What did she do?

ARD: Dumped me for my brother.

Pause.

I know it's dumb, but I feel like … if I find my other half—it'll complete me and then … I'll be happy. You know?

MANMATHA: You're not half Ard.
ARD: I'm half Aussie—half Indian.
MANMATHA: And that makes you very full. Very whole.
ARD: I don't feel whole.
MANMATHA: I do. Too much energy trapped in my body—ready to burst open like the hole in the dyke—god—sometimes I wish I could just spray my true essence everywhere like a whale's blow hole releasing the entire ocean from inside itself so it can breathe like the common mammal that it is.

    LIRAZ *enters.*

LIRAZ: A dingo stole my jalebi.

SCENE SIX

We are at Kollam's Rugby League Hall Of Fame Induction. CINDY *approaches* ARD. *They're just about to walk the red carpet.*

CINDY: Where is she?
ARD: She's coming.
CINDY: She better not stand you up.
ARD: She won't.
CINDY: Keep your arm around her waist at all times. Stay by her side. Make sure you kiss when they're taking photos. And when Kollam and the other players enter, make sure you're well off the red carpet.
ARD: Don't you want me in the group shots?
CINDY: I don't want you around the other players. I haven't managed to smooth things over as yet. And don't talk to the press. Especially if they ask about … you know what.

    ARD *sees* LIRAZ *enter. She's wearing a lovely outfit and has a handbag with her.*

ARD: Liraz is coming. Shhh.
CINDY: This is your brother's day Ard. I can rely on you, can't I?
ARD: I got this.

    ARD *moves to* LIRAZ *and kisses her suddenly and passionately.*

LIRAZ: Ooh.

ARD *holds her hand tightly.*

CINDY: Lorraine? So lovely to meet you!

LIRAZ: It's Liraz. Thank you for inviting me.

CINDY: Oh Ard—she's gorgeous. It's a tick from me! Leanne—I want you to meet Kollam. Ard—let's go and introduce Kollam to your new girlfriend.

> ARD *and* LIRAZ *move to the other side of the stage, alone.*
> BOYD, *a man in his 30s, enters looking very upset.*

LIRAZ: New girlfriend huh?

ARD: Sorry. She jumps to conclusions all the time.

LIRAZ: We'd need to have strict boundaries at work.

ARD: I got the job, did I?

LIRAZ: Obviously. You'll take it, won't you?

ARD: If I get to see you every day then that's the best job in world for me. Should we walk the carpet?

LIRAZ: Ahhh—

> CINDY *walks over to* ARD.

CINDY: [*looking at* BOYD] Who's that?

ARD: No idea.

CINDY: Is that a feather he has as an earring or a dream catcher?

ARD: I don't know.

CINDY: He better not eat any of the hors d'oevres. Tell him to piss off. This is a private event. Well go on!

> ARD *goes over to* BOYD. LIRAZ *stays with* CINDY.

ARD: Mate, this is a private event.

BOYD: I need to talk to you and Kollam.

ARD: Yeah, well, so do all these journos. Our press guy, Drayton's somewhere here—he can—

BOYD: I need to talk to you and Kollam, privately.

ARD: You can speak to our publicist if you need—

BOYD: It's about your dad.

> *Pause.*

ARD: What?

BOYD: I'm a friend of your dad's. We need to talk.

ARD: You mention my dad to me or my brother and we'll fucking … my brother's about to be inducted into the Rugby League Hall of Fame. Now would you kindly fuck off?
BOYD: I'm not leaving until you call Kollam over here.
ARD: That's not gonna happen. You need to leave. You want me to man handle you?

BOYD *snaps.*

BOYD: Yes! Maybe I do! Because the way you men have handled this situation makes me sick to my stomach!
ARD: What are you talking about?

DRAYTON, *the Hyperions' publicist, enters, bespectacled, in his 30s and reminiscent of Dominic Perrottet.*

DRAYTON: Where the fuck is Kollam?
ARD: He's outside having a fag.
BOYD: Please don't use that language.
DRAYTON: Who the fuck's this?
ARD: I have no idea.
DRAYTON: Well tell him to bugger off.
ARD: [*to* BOYD] Look—can you please just give me a minute?

BOYD *moves to the other side of stage.*

DRAYTON: [*to* ARD] Ard—we need to talk about your new girlfriend.
ARD: She's hot, isn't she?
DRAYTON: Haven't you read the papers? She's about to have her supposed metaphysical business exposed on *A Current Affair*!
ARD: What? Why?
DRAYTON: For ripping people off and for scamming stupid white people. She's charging two hundred bucks for a vial of holy drinking water from the Ganges. If people drank actual water from the Ganges they'd be poisoned. It's polluted as fuck. She's a scam artist Ard!
ARD: Don't say that, Drayton.
DRAYTON: Have you checked out her Twitter? She live-tweeted her time living in a monastery in Cambodia for months but she got business-class flights there and back!
ARD: She's not like that.
DRAYTON: How would you know? You've only just met her.

ACT ONE

ARD: Well you told me to bring someone.
DRAYTON: Not someone who's about to get cancelled on television! It's a PR nightmare! You can't be dating her!
   LIRAZ *moves over to* ARD *and holds his hand.* ARD *lets it go.*
BOYD: I'd like to make an announcement!
CINDY: [*to* ARD] I told you to get rid of him. You had one job!
BOYD: I'm a family member of Keeran Panicker's and—
DRAYTON: Who's Keeran Panicker?
CINDY: / He's my ex-husband.
ARD: He's my dad.
BOYD: I want to invite the Panicker family to a special event that will take place later this year. You've kept his name—so the least you can do is come to the scattering of his ashes / —
CINDY: / What?
BOYD: —which we'll be doing at the—
ARD: My dad's dead?
BOYD: Yes.
CINDY: [*upset*] No.
   BOYD *pulls out some flyers from his pocket and gives them to* ARD.
BOYD: Come to the scattering. The address and date is on the flyer. He would've wanted you there.
   ARD *throws the flyers into the air. Photographers start taking photos.*
LIRAZ: Ard.
   LIRAZ *picks up the flyers and puts them in her hand bag.*
CINDY: [*to the press*] Thank you all for coming here today. As you know I'm Kollam Panicker's mother Cindy Panicker, and I couldn't be prouder to induct my son into the Rugby League / Hall of—
BOYD: Hall of Hell! Where you Panickers belong!
CINDY: We may have lost the grand final this year but we are winners in every other—
BOYD: [*to* ARD] You killed him. You should all be ashamed of yourselves. What you did to Keeravani is unforgivable!

ARD *snaps.*
ARD: What he did to us was unforgivable!
CINDY: Ard let's go inside.
ARD: He was cruel!
BOYD: He was kind.
ARD: He was fucking cold!
BOYD: He was warm.
ARD: He used to beat me with a stick when I was a toddler to make me play footy. A huge stick!
CINDY: [*to the press*] It's hard living in the shadow of a successful relative. Just ask Dannii Minogue.
BOYD: Keeravani was an incredible man! Your toxic gladitorial world split him in two!
CINDY: Drayton.

DRAYTON *starts to physically drag* BOYD *away.*

ARD: He used to beat me and lock me in the cupboard with no water—no food! What sort of parent locks their child in a cupboard?!

CINDY, *feeling guilty and worried for* ARD, *embraces him.*

SCENE SEVEN

ARD *is on his front porch when* LIRAZ *approaches.*

ARD: Why haven't you been answering your phone?
LIRAZ: I'm sorry I had to run off.
ARD: Have you been crying?
LIRAZ: No. Yes.
ARD: What's going on?
LIRAZ: We need to forget these last few days ever happened. We have to pretend we never met.
ARD: I thought you wanted me to work at the spa with you?
LIRAZ: I do. But we can't. It's too hard. I'm going to the airport. My Uber's five minutes away.
ARD: I'll come with you.
LIRAZ: That's ridiculous.
ARD: I wanna be with you.

ACT ONE 23

LIRAZ: You don't even know me.
ARD: What about what happened yesterday?
LIRAZ: Fucking someone who's interviewing for a job is completely unprofessional. I'm sorry.
ARD: It was more than sex and you know it. Something happened to you.
LIRAZ: I have to go. I'll be late for my plane.
Beat.
ARD: Do you have any other Indian people working at the spa?
LIRAZ: I ... do I have any ... ? I've got all sorts of practitioners ... just not—well I—I've—we've ... you—
ARD: Were you only into me cos I'm brown and cos you needed brown people to work at the spa?
LIRAZ: That is a horrible thing to accuse me of.
ARD: Why wouldn't you get photos taken with me today? You worried they'll end up on *A Current Affair*?
LIRAZ: I'm in the wellness industry and I don't want to be seen in the sport section of *The Telegraph*. I should be in *Cosmo*. Or *Vogue*.
ARD: What's going on Liraz?
LIRAZ: My Uber's nearly here.
ARD: Why're you running away?
LIRAZ: I'm not running / away—
ARD: What happened to you yesterday?
LIRAZ: When you massaged me, I was transported somewhere, okay?!
ARD: Where?
LIRAZ: A stadium. I was transported to a stadium ... and all this foliage started to grow out from the seats, until the whole stadium became a forest. I walked into the forest and within seconds I was lost. But then this large blue bird appeared, a peacock, and it led me to a grove ... where I could make out two people. Naked. A man who looked like you, and a woman who looked like me. I wanted to get closer, but the blue bird called out—it made the most hideous noise and opened its plumage and shielded my view. I could hear them moaning in pleasure. Sucking. Fucking. But the peacock was completely blocking my eyes. So I got my lighter out and I torched that fucking bird. I set fire to it, and it screeched and flew away, and there they were ... in

all of their glory ... I could see all of them—and it was beautiful. Then there was a blinding flash and a sort of cracking sound as if lightning had struck right in front of me and the two people shot these rainbow coloured shards of light in all directions as if their auras were bursting. And then they kinda started melting ... morphing into one. I could smell sweat and sandalwood and ... sex. They morphed into some sort of creature—with this ... face. A painted face.

Beat.

Ard, before you massaged me, I hadn't had an orgasm in five years.
ARD: What? Why?
LIRAZ: Because I ... It doesn't matter.
ARD: Why couldn't you cum?
LIRAZ: It doesn't matter, it was just a blockage. But when I returned to my body, the blockage was gone. I'd had multiple orgasms—and I felt such ... clarity. And I realised ... my whole life is a lie. Building wealth by taking advantage of damaged middle-aged white women, teaching them how to astral travel when I don't even know how to astral travel myself. I don't know anything, anymore, except that that grove ... that face ... is enlightenment. And I need to go to India—to Kerala—to find it.
ARD: I'm coming with you.
LIRAZ: Under no circumstances will I allow you to come to Kerala with me. This is a journey I need to do alone.
ARD: I'm coming.
LIRAZ: You're staying. I want you to stay. Namaste.
ARD: What if I upgraded your flight? My family have a lot of points. Business-class astral travel?

LIRAZ kisses ARD.

SCENE EIGHT

MANMATHA *enters.* ARD, LIRAZ, GONDESHWAR *and* COREY *are present.*

MANMATHA: [*to the audience*] The alchemy of tantra involves a deep knowledge of one's own sexuality. A total control over sexual energy and the existence of pure and unconditional love. Totality that lies beyond duality. I need some volunteers in pairs.

ACT ONE

MANMATHA *points to audience members.* Twinkle you go with Hänsél. Alzbetta you go with Moss. Gondeshwar you go with Corey. Liraz, you go with Ard. The rest of the men in the class feel free to perform this on your wives and their precious yonis. Now—everyone, remove your clothing.

GONDESHWAR *and* COREY *remove their clothing.* LIRAZ *goes to remove hers.*

ARD: Liraz don't. [*To* MANMATHA] We're not comfortable taking our clothes off, Manmatha-ji.

LIRAZ: Speak for yourself.

MANMATHA: Very well Ard. Liraz, you can partner with me. Ard—you can sit this one out.

ARD *sits down, upset.* LIRAZ *removes her clothing.*

ARD: Why aren't you removing yours, Manmatha?

MANMATHA: A guru must always keep their sacred robes close to their temple—which is their body.

ARD: I don't think that's fair.

GONDESHWAR: If I was not naked, I would beat him for you Guru-ji. This behaviour is unprecedented.

MANMATHA: Relax Gondeshwar, concentrate on your yoni. Do not worry that Ard thinks I'm a phony.

GONDESHWAR: Your poetry always brings me to tears Guru-ji. If I had a thousand vaginas that turned into eyes, they would all be crying for you.

MANMATHA: Yes. Yes. Ard—would you like me to remove my clothes? You want to see me naked? Is that what you want?

ARD: Yep.

MANMATHA: Very well.

MANMATHA *removes his clothing.*

The yoni massage. The divine female passage. Start the massage by connecting her solar plexus chakra with the third eye. Do this by massaging her breasts and stimulating her nipples.

GONDESHWAR: Liraz? Why don't we swap?

MANMATHA: That won't be necessary Gondeshwar.
  Place your entire hand over her yoni.

MANMATHA *places his hand on* LIRAZ *and begins to massage her yoni. In the audience,* ARD *attempts to remain cool and collected, but eventually he explodes up to his feet.*

ARD: Stop!
LIRAZ: Ard, please don't.
ARD: Get your hands off her. Now! I'll be doing this massage. You instruct me.
LIRAZ: I'm sorry Guru-ji ... is it okay if ...
MANMATHA: It's quite alright Liraz. Friction is inevitable. Are you alright with him to take over?
LIRAZ: If you are—then yes.
MANMATHA: I'm alright with it Liraz. Ard, come and be Liraz's partner please. I'll stand next to you and instruct. You must be free also Ard.

ARD *nods and takes his clothes off too.*

I think we're all on the same page now. Where were we? Why don't we blindfold our models with a silk cloth?

ARD *blindfolds* LIRAZ, *and* COREY *blindfolds* GONDESHWAR.

Breathe. Deeply. Hold her yoni with a full hand. Hold it and vibrate. Massage lovingly the inner and outer labia. Lightly tickle the clitoris. Enter with one finger into the vagina making a come hither gesture. Press the G-spot firmly, massage in both directions ... Then, using your other hand, stimulate the clitoris. Breathe. When her body is fully charged with sexual energy she should clench and hold ... take three slow deep breaths ... clench her buttocks and abdomen and extend her hands and legs outwards. Sending energy out ... out ... out into the universe.

After reaching a peak close to orgasm under ARD's *hands,* LIRAZ's *breathing has slowed—she is peaceful and serene. She squeezes* ARD's *hand, and they share a moment.*

Remove your blindfolds. Swap places with your partners. Lie down. Put the blindfold on them now.

ARD *is blindfolded by* LIRAZ. COREY *is blindfolded by* GONDESHWAR.

The lingum massage. The divine phallus. Clasp your partner's penis in your hand, using plenty of oil. Begin a slow up and down motion … That's it. Goooood. Take the focus to his third eye, the sixth chakra. Breathe. Squeeze the base of the penis. Press down on the tip with your thumb. Bring him to the brink of ejaculation, but instead direct the orgasmic energy to the crown chakra and send that energy out of the top of his head. Breathe.

MANMANTHA *taps* LIRAZ *and signals for her to step aside.* LIRAZ *obeys. Blindfolded,* ARD *doesn't realise that it's* MANMATHA *now massaging him.*

Wet your index finger with oil. And for final kundalini awakening you will take three breaths and, on the third, insert a finger into the rectum to massage his sacred spot. On three.

MANMATHA *massages* ARD *and is just about to insert his finger.*

One. Two …

ARD *removes his blindfold.*

ARD: What the fuuuuuck?!

ARD *punches* MANMATHA.

GONDESHWAR: Guru-ji!
LIRAZ: Ard!
ARD: Fuck this! Fuck you! Fuck all of you!

ARD *grabs his clothes and exits.*

MANMATHA: There's something not right about that man. I can't put my finger in it.

SCENE NINE

ARD *runs to the ocean.*

LIRAZ: Ard. It's not safe to swim now!
ARD: I need to be in salt water!
LIRAZ: There's a huge rip.
ARD: Good. Let it take me!
LIRAZ: Please don't go in the water, Ard.
ARD: Why are you doing this to me?
LIRAZ: You're doing this to yourself.
ARD: He's fucking with me. Can't you see that?

LIRAZ: He's helping you.
ARD: By finger banging me in public?!
LIRAZ: It's okay that you enjoyed it.
ARD: You shouldn't have let him touch me!
LIRAZ: You're such a hypocrite!
ARD: What do you mean?
LIRAZ: I know why you left the Hyperions, Ard.
ARD: How could you know?
LIRAZ: I called the office. Spoke to someone called Waylon?
ARD: He's a fucking boofhead arsehole and he's full of shit. What Fuck Fragrance did to me was disgusting!
LIRAZ: Now you're being homophobic and it's not cool.
ARD: I'm not fucking homophobic! I grew up surrounded by men in short shorts who tackle each other a thousand times a week and shower together. I can't be homophobic! I just don't wanna be here! I'm losing my mind! I'm fucking falling in love with you, Liraz.

Pause.

I bought this down at the bazaar this morning.

ARD puts his hand into his pocket and pulls out a ring.

LIRAZ: Don't, Ard. Don't.
ARD: I love you.
LIRAZ: Ohhhh.
ARD: I know you love me too.
LIRAZ: I'm a lesbian, Ard.
ARD: What?
LIRAZ: I'm a raving dyke. Surely you knew that.
ARD: Why didn't you say something?
LIRAZ: I've got a girlfriend. Alli-Jane. We run the business together. You met her briefly at the job interview. She's gonna kick my arse when I get back home. And yours too probably.
ARD: But that's … No way you're a lesbian. What about all the fucking we did? Multiple orgasms? You said you hadn't cum in five years.
LIRAZ: I hadn't.
ARD: What about the grove?
LIRAZ: Oh—the grove.
ARD: What about the peacock?

LIRAZ: I don't know?! I'm sorry. / I'm so fucked up. I just—
ARD: What about the lighter—and you torching the bird's thingamajig?
LIRAZ: Five years ago I lost the love of my life. She was ... he was. He ... was everything to me. But he needed to be his true self. So he started to transition, he started taking hormones and slowly he changed ... from this soft, feminine person to this ... man ... next to me in my bed ... I tried. I really tried. And he could see that I was trying but ... I couldn't ... that's when I stopped cumming. When TJ left, I didn't cum for five years, even with Allie-Jane, my girlfriend. I had to fake it, every time, hating myself for it, because she is such a good person. She's given me so much—all the money to start up the spa! But then I met you. And you put your hands on me and I just ... I don't know what I'm doing here. But I can't love a man, Ard. I'm sorry. I just can't.

    GONDESHWAR *enters.*

GONDESHWAR: Guru-ji would like to see you in his hut, Ard. He extremely upset.
LIRAZ: Once Ard calms down, we'll both speak to—
GONDESHWAR: Guru-ji would like to see Ard. Alone. Now.

    ARD *and* GONDESHWAR *exit.*

    LIRAZ *takes out her phone and debates whether to call someone. She starts then stops, starts then stops again but eventually makes the call.*

TJ: [*voiceover*] Hello?
LIRAZ: TJ? Is that you?
TJ: [*voiceover*] It is.

    Toddlers can be heard crying in the background.

    Last mouthful Zeena. Come on. Pack your toys away Marcel or Daddy won't buy you an ice cream this afternoon. Sorry who's this?
LIRAZ: TJ. It's me.
TJ: [*voiceover*] Liraz. You've got a new number. It's been a long time.
LIRAZ: I miss you TJ. I just wanted to say I'm sorry. I know I hurt you. I keep hurting people. I'm a serial hurter—
TJ: [*voiceover*] Liraz. I'm about to request a video call with you. I need you to see my face when I say this. Okay?

LIRAZ: Okay.

    TJ*'s face appears on the subtitles screen.*

TJ: [*onscreen*] You leaving me was the best thing that ever happened to me. I've moved on. I've met the love of my life. We're married. We have two kids. I'm the happiest I've ever been.

LIRAZ: I've been with a guy TJ. That's crazy right? I'm a lesbian.

TJ: [*onscreen*] Liraz! Stop trying to apply hetero logic to everything It doesn't matter if you're bi or straight or a lesbian or whatever! You're so rigid! Just learn to bend.

    TJ *hangs up.*

    We are now in Manmatha's hut. He has several bottles of elixirs and a few tea pots on a table next to him. MANMATHA*'s lip is bleeding.*

MANMATHA: Close the door. Don't want any wild peacocks wandering inside. They make such an awful sound.

    ARD *closes the door. He and* MANMATHA *hold eye contact, each daring the other to talk.*

I've been a guru for thirteen years now and never have I ever been given a bleeding mouth by a student. Congratulations Ard.

ARD: You deserve it.

MANMATHA: You enjoyed it.

ARD: Punching you? Yes.

MANMATHA: You enjoyed me touching you. You enjoyed seeing me naked. You enjoyed our beach visit. You enjoyed walking the streets with your pinky entwined in Corey's. Have some tea.

ARD: Got anything stronger?

MANMATHA: I do. Have a small amount of this.

    MANMANTHA *hands* ARD *a strange-looking bottle.*

Just a tiny swig. It's very strong.

    ARD *drinks.* MANMATHA *takes a little sip too.* ARD *is taken aback by the strength of the elixir. He coughs and splutters as he catches* MANMATHA *also wincing at the strength of it.* MANMATHA *grins.* ARD *grins back.*

I want you to choose a name for Corey.

ACT ONE 31

ARD: I don't feel comfortable doing that.
MANMATHA: Choose him a new name and it will be his.
ARD: I don't know any Hindi or Malayalam.
MANMATHA: I named Gondeshwar after a crumbling little temple I drove past years ago. What shall we name Corey? Something silly? Piss cake? You name it—it's his.
ARD: You're funny.
MANMATHA: What about Ardha-Narish-Vara?

>MANMATHA *grins, provocatively.*

ARD: That's my name. It was on my birth certificate. My dad made me change it when I was a kid. How did you know?
MANMATHA: Rumpelstiltskin! Let's call Corey that!
ARD: How did you know?

>*There is the sound of distant cymbals and drums.* ARD *turns to the noise, which* MANMATHA *appears not to hear.* ARD *rubs his eyes—his tongue growing thick and his speech beginning to slur ...*

MANMATHA: You do know the story of Ardha-Narish-Vara right?
ARD: He's an Indian god.
MANMATHA: An Indian deity. And one that sprang from the—
ARD: Cheers to the many Indian deities!

>ARD *grabs the strange bottle from the table and downs all of the elixir.*

MANMATHA: Don't drink that—fuck.
ARD: Ever heard of rocket fuel? Me and the footy boys would always make it at footy camp. Mixing as many stiff drinks together so we could fuck ourselves up. Why don't I make us a special cocktail?

>ARD *pours all of the contents of the bottles into his mug.*

I name this cocktail ... Fuck Fragrance. Drink it.
MANMATHA: Shall we have some whisky instead?
ARD: Drink my Fuck Fragrance, Manmatha.
MANMATHA: I'll drink your Fuck Fragrance if you tend to my busted lip.
ARD: Very well.

ARD *holds* MANMATHA'*s eye contact, challenging—as he holds the cup outstretched.* Slowly, with trepidation, MANMATHA *accepts the cup. He takes a sip, nearly retching, then hands it back to* ARD. All of it.

MANMATHA *drinks the remaining contents of the cup.* ARD *follows through with his end of the bargain by placing his finger on* MANMATHA'*s bleeding lip and collects the blood.* ARD *opens his mouth to put his bloody finger in his mouth but last minute gives himself a tilak on his forehead.*

Corey left America cos he hates guns. He hoped that people would stand up for what's right—but they didn't. I looked in his phrase book and Sangram means revolution. Let's call Corey Sangram.

MANMATHA: You're good at naming people. You should stay here longer. Change your name back to what your father first intended. Or maybe you should be Sangram. You're a rebel deep down Ard— you've just been contained and you're waiting to break free. We can break free—you and I. Free ourselves from all of the meridians. You know Ard, many don't see it but Hindu mythology is filled with gender bending, queer stories. Arjuna, Ila, Shikhandi. Agni the god of fire would accept semen from the other gods. The essence of life.

ARD *puts his pinky out and* MANMATHA *slowly moves his hand to* ARD'*s.*

ARD: Manmatha-ji. Guru-ji. Finish the lingam.

ARD *pulls down his pants and underwear.* MANMATHA *spits on his finger and slowly inserts a finger into* ARD'*s rectum.*

The hut and MANMATHA *disappear, swallowed by darkness and the deafening sound of cicadas.* MANMATHA *morphs into* GAZZA, *a Hyperions Rugby League player dressed in a guernsey and only wearing a sports jock strap.* GAZZA *is limping and in pain.*

He gets on all fours on the massage table and arches his back towards ARD.

GAZZA: Aaaaargh! It hurts. It hurts. Awwwwwww.
ARD: I need you to stay still, Gazza.
GAZZA: I think it's my hip. I need you to stretch it. Owwww.

ACT ONE

    GAZZA *lies on his back and lifts his legs up.*
Help me Ard!
    GAZZA *bends his knees into his chest.*
Put your weight on me. Quick!
    ARD *crawls onto the massage table, lies on top of* GAZZA *and slowly puts his weight onto* GAZZA*'s knees.* ARD *leans over and kisses* GAZZA. *Black out. When the lights go back up,* GAZZA *has* ARD *thrown against the wall.* CINDY *enters.*

CINDY: We lost! We lost!

    GAZZA *and* CINDY *disappear into the darkness.*
    ARD *finds himself in a forest, naked.*
    We move into a montage of mini scenes.

I.

From the darkness, LIRAZ *emerges—dressed as a dancing peacock.* ARD *watches in wonder as she bursts into flames and disappears.*

II.

ARD *jumps, as a pair of hands appear on his shoulders.* CINDY*'s. She is dressed in Rugby League gear and begins to massage his shoulders. He leans into the massage, until* CINDY*'s hands travel up to his neck and begin to tighten around it.* ARD *tries to scream and thrash as* CINDY *chokes him. The moment he breaks free—*

III.

CINDY *transforms into* GONDESHWAR *covered in a thousand blinking eyes.* GONDESHWAR *grows larger and larger, and the eyes covering her body turn into vulvas—opening and closing.*

IV.

ARD *screams in terror and spins around to find a wall, inches from his face. He spins back to find another wall, also inches from his face. Trapped on all four sides,* ARD *begins to bash his fists against the wall. He is now five years old, whimpering like a small child.* ARD *now finds himself locked in a cupboard.*

ARD: Dadda?! Daddy! Dad!

ARD's face suddenly starts to twitch and convulse indicating the Kathakali facial expression of Bhayanakam. Lights snap to black then back up again. ARD *is gone and in his place is* ANAND, *dressed as* ARDHA-NARISH-VARA. ANAND *is adorned in a glorious costume. The outfit represents Lord Shiva and Goddess Shakthi combined—the feminine on the right and the masculine on the left—with a sharp rod still atop the head piece.* ANAND's *face twitches in exactly the same way* ARD's *face was twitching.*

ARD *finds himself sitting in the audience at the Kathakali amphitheatre.* MANMATHA *sits close-by.* LIRAZ *is also in the audience.* ARD *and* MANMATHA *are both drenched in sweat, breathing heavily, their pupils dilated.*

ANAND *speaks to the audience in English, with a thick accent. His face stops twicthing.*

ANAND: And they are the nine rasas—the nine emotions in Kathakali theatre. Rasa means essence. My name is Anand and I've been the owner of this dance theatre company for thirty years. Would you like to try the rasas with your own eyes? Come. The eyes must be lubricated with coconut oil every day in order to express the rasas. Open them widely. Good. Now move your eyes from side to side. Now move your eye brows up and down. Excellent. Now we are ready to begin.

Drums and cymbals accompany the performance, following the rising and falling tension of the story. KATHAKALI ACTOR (*holding a big percussive stick enters*) *and narrates the story whilst* ANAND *performs the dance.* KATHAKALI ACTOR *beats the stick on the ground to keep time as drums are heard. He speaks with an Indian accent.*

KATHAKALI ACTOR: One full moon, a male hunter stumbled across Goddess Shakthi and Lord Shiva making love in a beautiful forest grove. Goddess Shakthi was furious from being interrupted and declared that any living creature who entered the forest from then onwards would change sex. And so the hunter was transformed into a woman and found a husband who was a great sage that accepted him changing forms. The hunter switched back and forth as the moon changed—and the great sage made love to him, creating us all—the lunar dynasty.

MANMATHA: [*to an audience member*] It's a bisexual forest. A trans forest. Sorry.

MANMATHA stops himself from commenting any further.

KATHAKALI ACTOR: Even the trees and animals transformed back and forth to the other sex. Lord Shiva was so pleased by Goddess Shakthi's forest magic that he too wanted to change form—but Shakthi commanded that they join forces to be in a perpetual state of ecstasy. From this union sprung the avatar: Ardha-Narish-Vara! Half female. Half male.

ARD stands up from the audience. A yellow light shines on him as his face starts to contort and move into the Kathakali facial expression of Bhayanakam.

ARD: Rasa three: Bhayanakam. Terror!

ARD's whole body begins to twitch as his limbs begin to seize up.
LIRAZ comes down from the audience.

LIRAZ: Ard. What's wrong?

ARD walks on to the stage, stands in front of ANAND, then drops to the floor convulsing violently.

Is there a hospital around here?! Is there a doctor in the audience?!

ANAND holds ARD, hugs him, brings him to his feet, and the seizure stops.

[*To* ANAND] How did you do that? What did you do?

ANAND looks into ARD's eyes and recognises him as Keeran's son.

ANAND: Your eyes. Your eyes.

Suddenly MANMATHA *springs to his feet.*

MANMATHA: Ardha-Narish-Vara! You are the most beautiful of deities! [*To* ARD] And you are the wicked twitch of the west! But now I'm the one who's wicked. I'm the one who's melting. I have no business here on this spice trail! I shouldn't be here! Why are we here in this forest?! Thor! Where are you? Bring your hammer down on me! My viking ship has failed! Twelve meridians! Eight extra ones! Seven chakras!? Nine rasas!? Halves. Doubles. Triple nipples! How do we encapsulate our true essence?! Why must we be reduced? God?! You are an acronym! Generator. Operator. Destroyer!

MANMATHA *snatches* ANAND's *Kathakali headpiece and rips out the pointy sharp rod.*

ANAND: No!

MANMATHA *stabs himself in each chakra.*

MANMATHA: Chakra one! Chakra two! Chakra three! Chakra four! Chakra five! Chakra six! Chakra seven!

MANMATHA *dies when he stabs himself in the top of his head. Blackout. What the actual fuck?*

END OF ACT ONE

ACT TWO

SCENE TEN

Oil burners are situated on stage, with flames illuminating the walls and the audience. Two young Indian men appear, both shirtless, dressed in lungis and covered in coconut oil. They stare at each other, challenging each other. This is YOUNG MAN *and* YOUNG ANAND. *Drums begin to play.*

YOUNG MAN *and* YOUNG ANAND *engage in a highly physical and strenuous Kathakali training session—leaping from foot to foot, holding stress positions, at an ever accelerating rate. The coconut oil mixes with sweat, streaming down their bodies—as they continue to hold eye contact, daring the other to stop—and the drums push them faster and faster, joined by crashing cymbals.*

At the climax, the two men spin and turn to each other and each hold their own eyelids open with their fingers. They hold their eyes open for as long as they can, unblinking. As the whites of their eyes turn red, tears begin to stream down their faces. The drums and cymbals rise and crash and crash—until one of them breaks and closes his eyes. The moment he breaks—we plunge into darkness and the sound of cicadas.

From the dark, an image emerges: YOUNG MAN, *laying exhausted, still, with his eyes closed, in a grove, surrounded by flowers, milk, honey, and other offerings.*

SCENE ELEVEN

YOUNG WOMAN *enters wearing a backpack. She sees* YOUNG MAN *lying on the floor. She speaks with an Australian accent.*

YOUNG WOMAN: Are you alright?

    YOUNG MAN *sits up. He speaks with a thick South Indian accent.*

YOUNG MAN: I'm fine. I'm fine. Sorry to alarm you.

YOUNG WOMAN: I was about to call an ambulance. Or give you mouth to mouth or something.

YOUNG MAN: I need to unwind after each performance. Release the character from my psyche.
YOUNG WOMAN: That was you?
YOUNG MAN: It was.
YOUNG WOMAN: I didn't recognise you without all the make up.
YOUNG MAN: It's quite elaborate isn't it?
YOUNG WOMAN: It is. You're very strong.
YOUNG MAN: Thank you. I've been training here since I was a small child.
YOUNG WOMAN: It shows. I was absolutely mesmerised.
YOUNG MAN: Are you a dancer?
YOUNG WOMAN: I studied ballet but haven't really pursued it. Now I'm a cheerleader for my father's football club in Sydney.
YOUNG MAN: Ah. Australia. Where women glow and men chunder. That means vomit no?
YOUNG WOMAN: Very good. The men definitely do chunder. All of the men in my dad's football club are a pack of chauvinist arseholes.
YOUNG MAN: Well, the women definitely do glow.
YOUNG WOMAN: Flatterer.
YOUNG MAN: What was it that you liked about the show?
YOUNG WOMAN: Oh. Well … you were the best thing in it by far.
YOUNG MAN: Don't tell that to my colleague Anand. He plays god onstage and thinks he's god backstage too.
YOUNG WOMAN: He was good. But you as the goddess—I've never seen anything like it before. Such poise and … masculinity but such fierceness and femininity—you were vulnerable but grounded. And strong.
YOUNG MAN: Are you a reviewer?
YOUNG WOMAN: Oh. No. No.
YOUNG MAN: Are you from *Lonely Planet*?
YOUNG WOMAN: No. I'm just a tourist.
YOUNG MAN: Brave of you to come to India on your own. Are you … on your own?
YOUNG WOMAN: I am.
YOUNG MAN: You should be careful. It's not safe for a young girl like you to be alone. There've been reports of body snatchers and black tantric magic being practised here. Organs being stolen.

YOUNG WOMAN: I'm a big girl. I turned twenty-one last week. Spent it in Calcutta. Those Bengalis are wild. And quite frisky to be honest. Is that sweat on your body or oil?
YOUNG MAN: It's sweat. The oil is in my eyes. It helps lubricate them.
YOUNG WOMAN: You have very expressive eyes.

YOUNG MAN *stares at her deeply.*

YOUNG MAN: Would you like me to teach you some of the choreography? It's my very own.
YOUNG WOMAN: Really?
YOUNG MAN: Yes. I wrote the play myself too.
YOUNG WOMAN: I thought Kathakali plays were traditional.
YOUNG MAN: They are. But I've been trying to shift things. Why tell the same old god and goddess stories when you can create something new. It took years of convincing but ... it seems audiences are ready to see modern Kathakali stories. It's 1990. We need to keep up with the times.
YOUNG WOMAN: The merging of the god and goddess together was very powerful. And your portrayal of that deity afterwards—I can't pronounce the name—was just breathtaking. The duality. The grace.
YOUNG MAN: Ardha-Narish-Vara.
YOUNG WOMAN: Ard-huh-nourish-vara.
YOUNG MAN: Something like that.

YOUNG ANAND *enters but* YOUNG MAN *and* YOUNG WOMAN *don't see him.* YOUNG ANAND *is dressed in a lungi and is shirtless.*

YOUNG WOMAN: I just bought the most amazing table cloth with Indian deities painted on it.

YOUNG MAN *laughs.*

YOUNG MAN: Show me.

YOUNG WOMAN *opens her backpack and pulls out her tablecloth. It has tridevi (the triple goddesses) painted on it. She holds it up in front of* YOUNG MAN, *blocking their faces from each other. Then she innocently moves the tablecloth down. They both stare into each other's eyes.*

YOUNG ANAND *speaks in Malayalam.*

YOUNG ANAND: *Keeravani! Nammuk vyayamam cheyyam.* (Keeravani! We need to warm down.)

YOUNG MAN *answers back in Malayalam—they both speak in language as* YOUNG WOMAN *watches on. We see surtitles.*

YOUNG MAN: *Anand. Njan, Australiyayil ninnum vanna visitersinu kurach private dance class organise cheyyukayayirunnu.* (Anand. I was just organising some private dance classes for some Australian visitors.)

YOUNG ANAND: *Aashaan kuzhiyil ninnum enitt varum, ee kalaroopamthe nee kure vellakkarkkum thevarchhikalkum vendi nashippikkukayanegil.* (Master would turn in his grave if he knew you were bastardizing the art form for white tourists. And slutty ones too.)

YOUNG MAN: *Nammal ee kalaroopathe ipozhe malinamakkikkazhinju* ANAND. (We've already bastardized the art form Anand.)

YOUNG ANAND: *Athe, pakshe! Ithu nammudethanu malinamakkan. Avarukk tridevi yekkurich enthariyam?Ee meshaviriyil allathe? Avare ade kondoi adala kore ee British kaarude woosta-shit sauce oyikyum.* (Yes. But it's us. It's ours to bastardize. What does she know about tridevi except that it's on a tablecloth and soon to be covered in British breakfast Woosta-shit sauce!

YOUNG WOMAN: I should go. I just wanted to pop backstage and say how wonderful the show was. [*To* ANAND] Your performance was majestic. Thank you. [*To* KEERAN] I'm staying near the mermaid statue at the luxury huts on Mermaid Beach if you'd like to further discuss glowing and chundering.

YOUNG WOMAN *exits.*

YOUNG MAN: *Ee theatre onnu puthukki paniyanam. Njan ee sahip maruke class eduthaal namukkith puthukkipaniyanulla panam kittum Penne athil nammuk isttamulla pregadanagal undakkanum kalikkanum pattum.* (The theatre needs to be re-furbished. If I give classes to foreigners, we'll be able to afford an upgrade. And we can perform and create whatever plays we like, Anand.)

YOUNG ANAND: *Vannivide kidakku, nintte shareeram nalle vedana undarkyum.* (Come. Your muscles must be sore. Lie down.)

YOUNG MAN *lies down and splays his legs to the side with bent knees—spread eagle.* YOUNG ANAND *stands above him and begins to massage his thighs and groin with his feet, gently at first then quite vigorously.*

YOUNG MAN: *Pathiye. Ini njan cheyyam.* (Slow down. Let me do you.)
They switch places and YOUNG MAN *massages* YOUNG ANAND *with his feet.*

YOUNG ANAND: *Venda venda njan ninak thadavi tharum, njan cheyyam.* (No. No. I should do you. Let me do you.)
Green light shines on them for a moment. YOUNG ANAND *massages* YOUNG MAN *again.* YOUNG MAN *moves his facial muscles into the Kathakali dance facial expression of Bibhatsa.*

YOUNG MAN: Rasa four: Bibhatsa. Fear.

SCENE TWELVE

In the corridor of St Vincent's Hospital. CINDY *and* LIRAZ *stand at the doorway of Ard's hospital room.* CINDY *is blocking* LIRAZ's *entrance.*

CINDY: You need to leave.
LIRAZ: Cindy. Please. I think I know how to stop the fits.
CINDY: He's fine. There's no need to worry.
LIRAZ: He's in intensive care.
CINDY: And you're an intense nightmare.
LIRAZ: His mouth was frothing when the police separated us. I was so worried.
CINDY: You perverted him and took advantage of him. And then you left him in jail to rot!
LIRAZ: I tried to bail him out but my credit card wasn't working.
CINDY: Thank god the police finally saw that he had nothing to do with it. The press here mustn't find out about this. Do not tell a soul what happened—do you understand?
LIRAZ: It was in all of the papers in Kochin.
CINDY: Oh christ almighty! Drayton's gonna have a heart attack. The last thing this family needs is a media storm related to a cult suicide in India! *Woman's Day* mustn't find out about this! I've sold the rights of my wedding photos to them!
LIRAZ: It was in Yahoo news that Ard was in Saint Vincent's Hospital.

    DR LES *enters.*

DR LES: The fits have got worse. We need to give him more scans.

LIRAZ: I need to see him.
CINDY: Ard's told us all about you. Your whole life is a lie. Your business exploits vulnerable people and on top of that you're a bloody dyke! What the hell are you doing messing with my son?
LIRAZ: I love him. I think.

> ARD *walks into the corridor. He doesn't see* LIRAZ *at first. He's on a drip. His face twitching.*

CINDY: Go back to bed Ard. You need to be lying down.
DR LES: I'm taking him for an MRI. Come with me Ard.
CINDY: Go back to your room Ard. If you have another seizure you could injure yourself again.
ARD: Liraz?
CINDY: Go to your room!

> ARD's *body begins to convulse.* CINDY *and* DR LES *run to him.* ARD *calms down for a moment, still twitching.*

LIRAZ: I know how to help him. Ard, we need to go back to India—to that Kathakali dancer. He stopped your fit. He must be some sort of Kathakali healer.
CINDY: There is no way I'm letting you take him to another so-called healer!
LIRAZ: Then we'll bring the healer here. I'll pay to fly him here.
CINDY: With what? Your credit card?

> ARD *starts to cry.*

ARD: I never wanna see you again Liraz!
LIRAZ: But what about the grove? What about the grove Ard?
ARD: Get out! Get out! Don't contact us ever again! I hate you!

> ARD *falls to the floor and has a massive seizure and this time he can't breathe.* DR LES *holds him down.*

LIRAZ: Let me take him back to India, Cindy! He needs to go back to India!

SCENE THIRTEEN

ANAND *enters. He is on the phone.* LIRAZ *is standing on the other side of the stage.*

ANAND: You need to stop calling this number.
LIRAZ: Please Anand-ji. This is a life or death situation.
ANAND: I'm hanging up.
LIRAZ: Let me fly you to Sydney. Business class. I know you're a healer.
ANAND: I'm not a healer. I'm a kathakali dancer.
LIRAZ: You healed my friend. Ard Panicker. He was having a fit and your hands healed him—
ANAND: Panicker? I knew it!
LIRAZ: Knew what?
ANAND: I knew it was him! He's the splitting image of his father.
LIRAZ: Spitting.
ANAND: It's splitting.
LIRAZ: No it's spitting.
ANAND: I'm hanging up.
LIRAZ: Wait wait wait—Anand-ji—sorry. You knew Ard's dad?
ANAND: I knew it was his son. I could see it in his eyes.
LIRAZ: See what in his eyes?
ANAND: The curse. His father's curse!
LIRAZ: What curse?
ANAND: I knew if they'd return that it would be my downfall!
LIRAZ: What curse?
ANAND: His son returns to see his father's play and all hell breaks loose!
LIRAZ: Wait—Keeran wrote that play?
ANAND: They've closed my theatre.
LIRAZ: Why?
ANAND: That white man's suicide forced me to shut down my theatre. /
LIRAZ: / I'm sorry Anand-ji.
ANAND: / Thirty years I've been running it. And now I'm left with nothing. Just like I was thirty years ago!
LIRAZ: Ard's dad was a playwright?

ANAND: You tell Keeravani that I'm done performing his play! His family's cursed! I want nothing to do with Keeravani or his son!
LIRAZ: Anand-ji, Keeravani's dead.
ANAND: What?
LIRAZ: He's dead.
> Beat. ANAND *is devastated.*

ANAND: Kathakali has lost a great artist.
LIRAZ: Keeran was a Kathakali artist?
ANAND: How could you not know this? He was one of the greatest Kathakali dancers in Kerala. A genius. But he was cursed.
LIRAZ: By what? By who?
ANAND: Keeran was cursed by the deity he portrayed on stage. I'm telling you—that boy has the same curse. Stay away from that boy.
LIRAZ: How can I stop the curse, Anand-ji?
ANAND: I haven't seen Keeravani for thirty years. I don't know.
LIRAZ: Why was he cursed? Is that why he left India?
ANAND: I have to go.
LIRAZ: Is there a temple I can take him to? A temple of this deity?
ANAND: You would have to ask Keeravani.
LIRAZ: And how am I gonna do that?!
ANAND: Don't shout at me.
LIRAZ: Is there someone else who knew Keeran? Surely he had other friends?
> ANAND *hangs up.* LIRAZ *screams in frustration.*

It's spitting.

SCENE FOURTEEN

ARD *is standing with a drip in a large hospital gown. He's extremely weak.* CINDY *and* DR LES *are next to him.*

DR LES: We finally have the brain scan results back.
CINDY: And?
DR LES: They haven't shown anything.
CINDY: How is that possible?
DR LES: It's surprising I know. Honestly—I think it's psychosomatic. Sometimes illnesses are brought on by childhood trauma. Or recent

trauma. He needs therapy. We'd like to take him to see our in-house psychiatrist.

CINDY: *This* is what we've been waiting for? He nearly dies from not being able to breathe and you tell me he needs to see a shrink?! This is clearly a medical condition!

DR LES: I guarantee you—it's not.

CINDY: What about risperidone?

DR LES: Risperidone's not something I prescribe willy-nilly.

CINDY: This is not a willy-nilly situation doctor. I've been doing my own research and I believe that risperidone will cure him.

DR LES: It's the strongest anti-psychotic drug. Under no circumstance can it be prescribed for someone with no medical basis.

CINDY: Well—our Hyperions doctor does what I tell him and he's already got me a supply that'll last for months.

DR LES: I strongly object to that.

CINDY: I strongly object to keeping my son here any longer. I'd like him discharged immediately.

WAYLON *enters.*

We'll care for him at home and give him proper treatment. Come on Waylon—this guy's a dickhead. Let's find an actual doctor who knows how to discharge.

WAYLON: The press just arrived. They know Ard's here.

CINDY: Ard I told you to wear sunglasses when we went for a Paddle Pop!

ARD: I was convulsing. They wouldn't stay on my face.

WAYLON: It was a Golden Gaytime.

CINDY *storms out of the room followed by* WAYLON.

DR LES: I don't think you should listen to your mother.

ARD: Why?

DR LES: Those anti-psychotic drugs may suppress the fits—but the side effects will outweigh the benefits.

ARD: What are the side effects?

DR LES: You'll have absolutely no sex drive, you can say goodbye to having erections and there's a high chance you'll start growing breasts.

ARD *is horrified.*

ARD: I wanna get married doctor, I wanna have kids. Don't let my mum back in. I'd like to see your psychiatrist—

A loud alarm goes off over the loud speaker. NURSE *calls out to* DR LES.

DR LES: Wait here.

DR LES *runs out of the room.* Suddenly BOYD *bursts in, dressed in a nurse outfit.*

BOYD: You're Keeravani's son.

ARD: What are you doing in here?

BOYD: Just visiting a sick friend. What are you doing in here?

ARD: I'm asking myself the same question.

BOYD: You don't look well, man. Still handsome though. Got your dad's eyes.

ARD*'s eyes widen and his eyebrows start moving up and down.*

Did your dad teach you that?

ARD*'s face starts to convulse and his whole body starts shaking.*

Shit.

ARD*'s fit escalates.*

NURSE: [*off*] He's in this room!

Not knowing where to hide, BOYD *dives under* ARD*'s hospital gown and wraps himself around* ARD. *Time and space bends for a moment and the grove begins to appear.*

DR LES *enters and we're back to reality. The grove disappears.*
BOYD *is face to face with* ARD—*still in* ARD*'s hospital gown, his body wrapped around* ARD*'s body. They hold eye contact.*

Then, BOYD *sees the doctor and runs out of the room.* ARD *has an erection and sits down, covering his crotch.*

DR LES: I'm so sorry about that. Right, where were we? That's right. I can book you in to see our psychiatrist right away.

ARD *is ashamed that* BOYD *gave him an erection.*

ARD: Doctor, I've changed my mind. I'm gonna go home with my mum. I'd like to be discharged.

SCENE FIFTEEN

LIRAZ *is in a hospital room with* NURSE NICK. *She has her handbag with her.*

LIRAZ: So this was his room?
NURSE NICK: He died right there.
LIRAZ: Did he ever talk about a … curse?
NURSE NICK: He barely spoke to anyone. Such sad eyes.
LIRAZ: Did he ever have fits?
NURSE NICK: I can only give that sort of information to family members.
LIRAZ: I'm his niece.
NURSE NICK: Really?
LIRAZ: Yes. Now did anyone ever visit him?
NURSE NICK: There was a guy. He'd visit all the time.
LIRAZ: Who was he?
NURSE NICK: You'll need to prove that you're a Panicker if I'm to tell you that.
LIRAZ: Look. I'm the proprietor of Shakthi Health Spa in Bondi. I could offer you as many free treatments as you like if you—
NURSE NICK: Shakthi Health Spa? Oh my god. My girlfriend's been going there since you opened. What did you say your name was?
LIRAZ: Li … La-vosh. Lavosh.
NURSE NICK: Lavosh? As in lavosh bread?
LIRAZ: My mother had cravings for lavosh bread when she was pregnant with me so she named me after her favourite bread.
NURSE NICK: How inspiring. I think I'll call my kids Pumpernickel and Naan. Seriously though, your spa—it saved my girlfriend's life. She'd been unwell for years. Self harming. It was awful. We tried everything but she just couldn't pull herself out of her depression. Then she tried your astral-travel classes and suddenly she was able to look at herself and the world from a new perspective.
LIRAZ: I'm so glad my classes helped her.
NURSE NICK: Honestly. She adores you. You have a true gift Lavosh. You're a healer.
LIRAZ: Thank you.

NURSE NICK: Wait till my girlfriend finds out that Lavosh Panicker is giving her unlimited spa treatments!
LIRAZ: Lucky girl. Now can you tell me about this guy that visited Keeran?
NURSE NICK: His name was Boyd. We all thought he was his therapy nurse but … he wasn't.
LIRAZ: What was he?
NURSE NICK: From what I gathered when we were chatting at the urinal—he's a witch.
LIRAZ: What?
NURSE NICK: A male witch.
LIRAZ: How can I find him?
NURSE NICK: Dunno.
LIRAZ: Well you're just fucking useless aren't you?
NURSE NICK: And you're full of shit. Out!

NURSE NICK grabs LIRAZ's arm and tries to lead her out. LIRAZ pulls away and starts to hit him with her hand bag. Suddenly she remembers something. She opens her hand bag and empties its contents onto the floor. Essential oil facial spritzers, tampons and way too many Rescue Remedy sprays fall out.

Lavosh. You're not Keeran's niece. Are you?

LIRAZ does one final, frantic search of the hand bag and pulls out the flyers she collected from BOYD in Act One. She holds them like a prize.

That's a lot of Rescue Remedy.

She sprays some Rescue Remedy in her mouth.

LIRAZ: Told you I'm a panicker.

SCENE SIXTEEN

WINSOME, *a denizen of the Body Somatic, stands in a slightly grubby-looking rec room. She's holding a blade and a chalice. Dotted around the room are the denizens of the Body Somatic—men, women, queer, trans and non-binary people half-dressed in wild, colourful dress-ups, with bright face-paint and smeared fistfuls of glitter. Oversized sequin dresses hanging off thick, hairy bodies … jockstraps, breasts.*

ACT TWO

WINSOME: We'll now perform The Great Rite. The goddess and the god coming together. If you don't want to use the blade and chalice, you're most welcome to use your own bodies, or your hands, or a chopstick in a bottle of wine. Whatever works for you. Now—let us see if we can make contact with our QUEEN.

>WINSOME *clears their throat.*

We call upon the goddess and god and feel their love.

>WINSOME *places the blade inside the chalice three times. She suddenly gasps.*

Oh. I wanna dance with somebody. I wanna feel the—

>*Suddenly* LIRAZ *enters holding the flyers.*

LIRAZ: Sorry to interrupt. I'm looking for a … witch called Boyd?

>*Everyone starts laughing.*

WINSOME: Boyd!

>BOYD *enters wearing only his jocks.*

LIRAZ: I'm so sorry to interrupt your … séance Boyd, but … I need your help. I need to reverse a curse. To make contact with a deity.

>*Everyone starts laughing.*

What's so funny?

WINSOME: You've come to the right place.

LIRAZ: I have?

WINSOME: We're contacting a deity right now.

LIRAZ: Who?

WINSOME: Whitney.

>*Music blasts through the speakers and everybody begins to cheer and dance.*

>LIRAZ *is now thrashing to music with a bottle of wine.* BOYD *dances with her. The music is lowered as they speak.*

LIRAZ: I can't believe Kylie Minogue has her own wine label. The rosé's actually really good.

BOYD: Should we open another bottle?

LIRAZ: Yes we should.

BOYD *opens another bottle and pours.*
LIRAZ: Nurse Boyd—
BOYD: Please don't call me that.
LIRAZ: Sorry. Pink Floyd—you're a really good guy. I feel like I've been part of the Body Somatic for years.
BOYD: They have a way of welcoming newcomers, hey? When Keeranvani and I first came here it was like a homecoming.
LIRAZ: How does a small witchy somatic group stay afloat in exorbitant Sydney?
BOYD: They were struggling to pay rent to be honest, so I bought the building and now it's all donations based.
LIRAZ: Bought?! Are you rich Boyd?
BOYD: My parents were.
LIRAZ: So now you're King of the LGBTs.
BOYD: Queen.
LIRAZ: Queen of the LGBTQIs! All the colours of the rainbow! Wait—did I leave out a letter?
BOYD: LGBTQIA-plus.
LIRAZ: A plus! I was always an A plus girl at school. Are you the G? No—you're the B! Asexual? No. You can't be. You're the plus, aren't you? What does the plus stand for?
BOYD: Sexuality is limitless Liraz.
LIRAZ: I dunno. Limitless is a cop out. What does that even mean?
BOYD: Not everything can be defined Liraz. Gender is limitless too.
LIRAZ: I'm a woman and I like women.
BOYD: Great. But—what if ... the moment you decide ... is the moment you're trapped.
LIRAZ: Boyd—
BOYD: It's delicious to surrender to it all. Keeravani called it shapeshifting. I'm definitely a Q-plus student.
LIRAZ: Queer shmeer. I know straight guys in Bondi who call themselves queer because they wear orange nail polish. Orange nail polish doesn't make ya queer, honey. I'm the L. I'm definitely a lesbian.
BOYD: Good for you. It's good to be sure about who you are.

    LIRAZ *kisses* BOYD.

What are you doing?

LIRAZ: I … don't know.
BOYD: L for Liraz. Just be you.
LIRAZ: I'm so sorry.
BOYD: It's okay. Do you want another joint?
LIRAZ: No! Oh god. I'm trashed. Is it bad to make contact with a deity when you're trashed?
BOYD: Whitney didn't seem to mind. Should we do another Great Rite ritual and call upon the deity who's name I can't seem to pronounce.
LIRAZ: I can't pronounce it either.
BOYD: Probs best to be able to say the name properly if we're calling on them.
LIRAZ: Shit. Wait! We need Ard. We can't reverse the curse without Ard.
BOYD: We could all rock up to the hospital and do it there?
LIRAZ: He's back at his mum's house.
BOYD: Well let's go there.
LIRAZ: We can't. He doesn't wanna see me again.
BOYD: Well what are we gonna do?
LIRAZ: I have an idea.

Lights fade on LIRAZ *and* BOYD.

ARD *is in his bedroom wearing a dressing gown.* CINDY *bashes on the door.*

CINDY: Ard—the Hyperions doctor's still waiting downstairs. He's got your first course of medication, sweetheart. Ard?

She bangs on the door again.

You okay love? Open the door. You alright? Shit! Kollam! I think he's having another fit. Kollam! Why are you never bloody well here when we need you?! Waylon! I need you to knock the door down.

ARD *clearly doesn't want to open the door. He looks for an escape. Suddenly his cupboard door opens and a portal appears.* ARD *enters the cupboard. The world shifts again.* CINDY *turns into* GONDESHWAR, *dressed as a spiritual air hostess.*

GONDESHWAR: Welcome to your business-class astral flight. I am your purser Gondeshwar. Please take seat and sit on your strap-on. I mean—please sit and strap yourselves on. In. You want to go up in astral? Sit your ass down. We hope you enjoy your medi-ta-ta-tive flight on *Air Strap Ommm.*

LIRAZ *and* BOYD *enter. They're both drunk and stoned.*

Welcome on-board Air Strap Ommm. Please take your seat.

BOYD: It worked Liraz. You did it.

GONDESHWAR: Please strap yourselves in. On.

LIRAZ: There are no seat belts.

GONDESHWAR: Then we can only hope there be no turbulence. Prepare for jack-off.

LIRAZ: I think you mean take-off.

GONDESHWAR: Thank you for correction. Nice girl. Pretty girl. Prepare for fuck off.

They launch into the astral plane.

LIRAZ: Did you bring the blade and the chalice?

BOYD: No.

LIRAZ: Boyd. That's the whole point of us doing this. Isn't that the only way to activate The Great Rite?

BOYD: There are other ways.

GONDESHWAR: You two like married couple. I'm celebrant also. Want me to marry you in air?

LIRAZ & BOYD: No.

LIRAZ: It's business class yeah? We'll order two glasses of Vintage Dom Perignon.

GONDESHWAR: Air Strap Ommm only serve Kylie Minogue Rosé.

BOYD: You did say you liked it.

ARD *enters through the closet.*

GONDESHWAR: Air Strap Ommm requires all passengers to take a shit.

BOYD: I think you mean seat.

LIRAZ: Ard!

ARD: Liraz?

ARD *embraces* LIRAZ. *It's a gorgeous reunion.*

LIRAZ: I'm so, so sorry about what happened in India. Manmatha fooled us all. He completely sucked me in.

ARD: He completely sucked me off.

ACT TWO 53

They both laugh. GONDESHWAR *laughs loudly.*

ARD: Gondeshwar? I'm surprised you didn't move back to Eastern Europe.

GONDESHWAR: When ashram shut down I went undercover and moved to New Zealand. There I learnt how to do kiwi accent.

She changes her accent to a New Zealand one.

Life was fin-tis-took so I bought a truck, learnt how to drive around New Zealand giving mobile tantric massages. And I called my business tin-truck.

ARD *starts to laugh.* GONDESHWAR *exits. Suddenly* ARD's *face moves into the Kathakali dance expression of Hasyam. Purple light shines on him for a moment. For the first time the facial twitch is a joyful experience for* ARD. ARD *continues to laugh.*

ARD: Hasyam! Rasa five: Hasyam. It's one of the nine rasas in Kathakali dance. I don't know how I know that but I do.

BOYD: [*to* ARD] God you have a beautiful smile.

LIRAZ: Ard. You know Boyd.

ARD: Are you really a nurse?

BOYD: Technically, no.

ARD: So what are you? How did you know my dad?

Pause.

Oh my god you're a prostitute.

BOYD: I'm an aged care sex worker.

LIRAZ: And a witch too. A good witch. A white witch.

BOYD: A brown witch.

ARD: You were fucking my dying dad?

BOYD: Not fucking. We'd make love.

ARD: I don't wanna know about my dad making love to a sex witch!

ARD *stands up and moves to the other side of the plane.* GONDESHWAR *enters with Kylie Minogue Rosé. She pours it for her passengers.*

GONDESHWAR: I preferred South Island to North Island but people soon realised that kiwi accent not my natural voice and in my tin-truck people on South Island got very mad when massage moved down south. So my tantric tin-truck was shut down which gave me no choice but to become air hostess.

GONDESHWAR *looks at* ARD.

GONDESHWAR: Panicker. You looking very pale. You need food. Time for food service! Air Strap Ommm also employ me as human buffet—food served on me. I'll prepare to be wheeled on.

GONDESHWAR *exits*.

LIRAZ: Ard. The fits are a curse. You have the same curse as your dad. How do you pronounce the deity we saw in the Kathakali play?

ARD: Ardha-Narish-Vara.

LIRAZ: Yes. You've been cursed by that deity. And Boyd and I are gonna perform a ritual called The Great Rite to try and reverse a curse. Except Boyd forgot to bring the tools that activate the ritual.

GONDESHWAR: [*off*] Wheel me on!

ARD: What's the Great bloody Rite?

BOYD: It's a ritual. We usually use a blade and a chalice—click them together three times. It's symbolic intercourse.

GONDESHWAR: [*off*] Food is ready!

BOYD: But sometimes it can be sex magick.

ARD: Oh god!

BOYD: Two bodies becoming one in ritual in order to bend and shape their destinies. It's like a physical way of saying amen or so mote it be—it's like a prayer. Madonna knew.

ARD: What the bloody hell does so mote it be mean?

BOYD: It's an ancient pagan way of saying amen.

ARD: My dad was a Hindu.

BOYD: Yes—but he called upon so many other deities from different cultures. Our Body Somatic classes have Buddhist and Wiccan and Christian and Atheist students. All sorts of people—men, women, trans people, non binary. Everyone loved Keeravani. He had access to all sorts of deities. Not just Indian ones. He facilitated so many Great Rite rituals.

ARD: This is so wrong.

BOYD: How can the Great Rite be wrong?

GONDESHWAR: [*off*] Could someone wheel me on?!

ACT TWO

BOYD: Keeravani changed so many people's lives Ard. Inspired so many of us. Especially people of colour. Body positive, sex positive people. Free of colonial guilt and shame.
GONDESHWAR: [*off*] Dinner service is ready!
BOYD: Hundreds of people will be attending his ashes scattering. You need to be there too. I have so much I wanna pass on to you.
ARD: I'm sure you do—chlamydia for starters.
LIRAZ: Ard—we need to perform the Great Rite now. We need to invoke Ardha-narish-vara.
BOYD: Shit. We forgot to bring offerings. It's always best to make offerings to deities. [*Gasping*] We can offer the Kylie wine!
LIRAZ: I drank it all.
BOYD: Liraz! What are we gonna offer the deity now?

> GONDESHWAR *enters, near naked with food stuck on to her body.* BOYD *and* LIRAZ *stand on either side of her and put their hands on her shoulders.*

We bring you this offering direct from South Island!
GONDESHWAR: What you waiting for? Eat me!

> *Suddenly there's terrible turbulence. The plane drops.*

We experiencing turbulence. Please take seat. And let masks of oxygen go down on you!

> *Three oxygen masks come down from the ceiling—a jock strap, a skimpy undie mask and a bdsm puppy mask.* BOYD, ARD *and* LIRAZ *put them on.*

Eat from your human buffet!
ARD: I need to get off this plane.
GONDESHWAR: Come Liraz! Come eat with Strap Ommm pilot. I take you to cockpit.

> *The plane dives.*

BOYD: Liraz! This is your astral plane. You need to fly it.
LIRAZ: I don't know how!
BOYD: I believe in you Liraz. I believe in you.
LIRAZ: Where's the pilot room?

> GONDESHWAR *points both thumbs to the food covering her groin.*

You've got to be kidding me.
GONDESHWAR: Stupid girl! Your shitty astral travel airline more dodgy than Jetstar! Air Strap Ommm is goin' down! Prepare for landing!

Utter chaos ensues. LIRAZ *dives into* GONDESHWAR's *groin.* ARD *runs back into the cupboard.*

SCENE SEVENTEEN

ARD *is alone in a bathroom, staring at himself in a mirror. Outside, the dull thud of techno music.* ARD *breathes in and out, psyching himself up. His face starts to do a small twitch. He takes a handful of pills from his pocket and swallows them. He slaps himself in the face—psyching himself up.*

Then in a snap we are in a private VIP room at a club, with a stripper, JOJO, *dancing for* WAYLON, *and* GAZZA *snorting a huge line off a mirrored table.* GAZZA *sits away from the other two.* WAYLON *is dressed in drag wearing a wig with condoms tied to it.* GAZZA *wears a wig and a feminine kimono.*

WAYLON: [*to* ARD] When was the last time you and Gazza saw each other?
ARD: Who wants another round of shots?
GAZZA: Fuck yeah!
WAYLON: Gazza. Come and sit with us.
GAZZA: Nah. I'll stay over here ay?
WAYLON: It's my round. What do we want? Quick fucks? Slippery nipples?
GAZZA: You and me—let's have sambucca shots Waylon. But you should get Ard a cock-suckin' cowboy.
ARD: I'll get this round.
WAYLON: It's my shout.
GAZZA: Nah Waylon! It's ya bucks night. You're not payin' for nothin.'
WAYLON: I've got it.

WAYLON *goes to get the drinks. There's an awkward silence between* ARD *and* GAZZA. ARD *pulls out some pills from his pocket and swallows them.*

GAZZA: Is that ecstasy?
ARD: Yeah. Nah.
GAZZA: I'd double dump if I didn't have to play. Or back door it. Fucking drug tester cunts.
ARD: I can't hear you Gazza. Why don't you come and sit here.
GAZZA: Yeah. Nah.

Another awkward pause.

You excited about the wedding?
ARD: I'm pumped. It's gonna be great to see all the boys again. Get shit aced like the good old days.
GAZZA: Yeah. Ya lucky to have Waylon in ya family. He's like a father to us all.
ARD: Yeah. I've scored a pretty awesome stepdad, ay? Winner winner chicken dinner.
GAZZA: Yeah. We'll win next year's premiership for sure.
ARD: Up the mighty Hyperions!
GAZZA: Your mum's segment on the Footy Show is so fuckin' brilliant. She's hot too.
ARD: Thanks.
GAZZA: Do you want jugs?
ARD: Jugs of beer?
GAZZA: No dick head. Her jugs. Jojo's jugs.

GAZZA *stares at* JOJO.

ARD: She's pretty hot.

JOJO *smiles at* ARD. ARD *moves over and sits next to* GAZZA.

Garry ... I'm sorry about what happened.
GAZZA: Let's not go there mate.
ARD: I don't know what came over me.
GAZZA: We lost man. We lost.

GAZZA *starts crying.*

I'm sorry you got fired.
ARD: I just want you to know that that's never happened before.
GAZZA: We don't need to talk about it. Look every now and then I don't mind a quick game of Soggy Sao with the boys but getting kissed by ya footy physiotherapist during a treatment—not on.

ARD: I'm sorry Gazza.
GAZZA: You had a stiffy when you kissed me, didn't ya?
ARD: I was looking at the Playboy calendar on the wall and ... I just got carried away. Miss July had amazing jugs. It was completely unprofessional and ... I'm ashamed.
GAZZA: That calendar's pretty hot. It's been in the change room since the eighties. It's been on Miss July for as far back as I can remember. The pages are all stuck together. Ha! Iconic. I'm sorry I punched you in the face.

WAYLON *returns with the shots.*

ARD: Waylon!
GAZZA: Up ya bum!
WAYLON: Up ya bum.

They drink the shots.

GAZZA: Where are all of the other fellas?
WAYLON: They're in the booths or upstairs.
GAZZA: Ahhhh. Hahahaha.
ARD: Waylon, I'd really like to start playing reserve grade.
WAYLON: I don't think that's a good idea Ard.
ARD: I feel really good now thanks to you and Mum. Stronger. Fitter.
WAYLON: I don't think the other fellas would be too comfortable if you play with us—not since ...
GAZZA: I'm gonna go play the pokie pokies.

GAZZA *exits.*

ARD: Does everyone know that you fired me or do they think that I quit?
WAYLON: Gazza told everyone what happened. Ya reputation's shot mate.
ARD: I can prove to the boys that I'm one of them. I've always been one of them. It was just one slip up. I wasn't thinking straight.
WAYLON: Clearly.
ARD: Let me prove it to you Waylon. I want you and Mum to be proud of me. The way you are of Kollam. Lemme play reserve grade and I'll show you how good I can be.
WAYLON: If you wanna play with the big boys you gotta show me that you're up for it. Obviously ya good with balls but will ya put ya body on the line?

ARD: What do you mean?
WAYLON: [*to* JOJO] JoJo!
JOJO: More shots Waylon?
WAYLON: Is there a booth free now darlin?
JOJO: Sure is.

> JOJO *walks over to* ARD *and* WAYLON. WAYLON *gives her a huge wad of cash.*

[*To* ARD] Are you as well-endowed as your brother?

> JOJO *leads* ARD *into a sex booth.*

WAYLON: I'll wait outside.

> JOJO *locks the door from the inside with a key and slips it under the door to* WAYLON. WAYLON *exits.*

JOJO: You're not like those other boofheads. I can tell. Do you wanna fuck me or do you wanna make love?

> JOJO *puts her hand on his crotch.* ARD *pushes her hand away, frustrated as the world starts to bend.*

Plenty of things we can still do when it's soft.
ARD: Can we just sit opposite each other and look into each other's eyes? Rock a bit?
JOJO: I mean we could.
ARD: Why did you bring me here Liraz?
JOJO: My name's JoJo but you can call me Liraz if you like?
ARD: Why did you lock me in here Mum?
JOJO: Mum? Okay. Incest fantasy. More common than people realise.

> ARD *begins to lose his mind.*

ARD: Let me out of here! Let me out Mummy!
JOJO: Okay, this is too much. I can't do this.
ARD: Daddy! Dad! Let me out! Let me out!

> ARD *is now on the floor screaming like a hysterical child.* JOJO *goes to the door.*

JOJO: Let us out, Waylon. It's not happening. Waylon open the door.
WAYLON: [*off*] Not until you do what I paid you to do.
JOJO: Oh for fuck's sake.
ARD: Aaaaaaaaaargh! Let me out! Let me out!

ARD runs to the door and starts to bash it down.
JOJO: Just open the door Waylon!
ARD: Open the door Mummy! Please! Please! Mummy! Mum!
From the other side of the door, muffled at first, we hear CINDY *and* KEERAN's *voices—shouting. Through the darkness they appear—younger and in mid-nineties costumes.*
KEERAN: I didn't do anything wrong!
CINDY: You're disgusting!
KEERAN: What's disgusting about it?
CINDY: Have you been doing this with Kollam?
KEERAN: No. Kollam prefers to kick the ball in the park.
CINDY: Why can't you do that with Ard?
KEERAN: I will. I promise.
CINDY: No. I don't want you going near him anymore.
KEERAN: He's my son.
CINDY: Stay away from him Keeran. I mean it. And if you touch him again I'll fucking kill you.
KEERAN: I didn't touch him Cindy. I would never—
CINDY: I don't wanna hear another word Keeran. It's unnatural and disgusting!
KEERAN: How can you say that? How can you be the same woman I met?
CINDY: He's a child Keeran! He's a child.
KEERAN: And we have to let him express himself.
CINDY: This has to stop. All of it. No more.
KEERAN: But I'm setting up the school—
CINDY: With my money.
KEERAN: I wouldn't have come out here if I knew—
CINDY: It has to stop. Set up the school. I'll give you the money but I want you to move out.
KEERAN: What do you mean?
CINDY: I don't want you living under this roof with my boys. How much do you want?
KEERAN: You can't pay me to leave my boys.
CINDY: I'll pay you as much as you want. You could go back to Kerala and start a new school.
KEERAN: I can't go back to India.

CINDY: Were you ever attracted to me Keeran?
KEERAN: Cindy—
CINDY: Was I just an escape route for you? I did love you. Truly. But this has to stop. I'll put half a million dollars into your account if you disappear. You could send some of the money back to your family.
KEERAN: Please don't make me do this.
CINDY: You want your son to get teased? To get bashed? To get murdered? Haven't you heard about the men going missing from the Bondi cliffs?
KEERAN: Cindy please.
CINDY: Do this. For him.
KEERAN: Give me the key. Give me the key Cindy!
CINDY: Leave him in there.

> KEERAN *and* CINDY *exit.*
>
> ARD *resumes shouting and banging on the door of the cupboard.*

ARD: Daddy!? Dad!!?

> ARD *breaks down the door. He tumbles from the closet in* CINDY*'s house onto the floor.*

Why did you lock me in the cupboard?!
CINDY: I was trying to protect you!
ARD: I was screaming for you all night! All night! Why did you do that to me?!
CINDY: Because I was scared of what he would do to you!
ARD: Tell me what he did?!
CINDY: It's one a.m. I'm going back to bed.

> CINDY *tries to leave.*

ARD: Tell me or I'll tell *Woman's Day* that Cindy Panicker's loser son begged a cult leader in India to shag him!
CINDY: I knew this would happen. This is all my fault. I allowed it.
ARD: Allowed what?
CINDY: I allowed him to teach you his choreography.
ARD: Dad was a dancer?

> ARD *suddenly remembers. He gasps through tears of joy.*

Oh my god I remember. I loved his choreography.

CINDY: It was fine when you were little and dancing around the house. But then he started dressing you in skirts and bells and putting make up on you. Like you were some sort of ... a five year old should not be dressed in drag! And now look at you!

ARD: I remember. I loved it. More than anything. I loved him.

CINDY: I wanted you to play sports like your brother. The culture of footy is what binds this country together.

ARD: I begged dad to dress me up! I was the one who made him buy me the costumes. I instigated all of it. Oh my god. That stick. He never beat me with it. He used it to keep time to the drum beat while I danced. I just wanted to dance like him. I was good at dance Mum. But you made me play footy. I've been raised by boofheads. And now I'm a mess. You've made me a mess.

CINDY: I've given you every opportunity under the sun. You've had every chance to succeed.

ARD: You've been trying to drug me.

CINDY: I've been trying to help you! You can't blame me for everything!

ARD: Yes I can!

CINDY: Stop barking at me. I wish I'd kept my anti dog barking device after Zsa Zsa got run over. I'd zap you right now.

ARD: Why'd you stop me dancing?

CINDY: I didn't want life to be hard for you. Your brother was naturally confident but you were so timid.

ARD: He's white like you—the fair-skinned son. That's why he was confident.

CINDY: I didn't want you to be mocked. Kathakali shifted the way you held yourself. The way you walked and gestured. Boys at school were teasing you. The footy parents were all gossiping. It was hard enough for you being the only brown kid at school—I couldn't let them ridicule you over this as well. You came home crying all of the time saying the boys were calling you blackie. It broke my heart. I couldn't change your skin colour but I could change this.

Pause.

Waylon will let you play reserve grade Ard. It's a great salary. It'll keep you fit and healthy. Life will be so much easier. I love you Ard. I truly do. I know what's best for you. Come on.

He yields like a child and rests his head on her chest.
I need you at my wedding my darling. More than anything in this world. I want you to walk me down the field. Will you walk me down the field?
ARD *is silent. He nods.*
I need to get this off my chest though darling.
ARD *moves his head off her chest.*
Not you off my chest. Your father wrote to you and Kollam for years—but I destroyed the letters. I'm sorry. Truly. Will you forgive me?
Blue light fills the stage for a moment as ARD*'s eyes widen and his face moves into the Kathakali dance facial expression of Raudram.*
ARD: Rasa six: Raudra. Wrath.

SCENE SEVENTEEN

The Panicker house disappears and ARD—*breathless and heaving is now outside Shakthi Health Spa. A large sign reads 'CLOSED UNTIL FURTHER NOTICE'.* ARD *bangs on the door.*

ARD: Liraz. Liraz! Boyd!
The Shakthi Spa door slowly opens.

SCENE EIGHTEEN

ARD *is preparing his massage table for the Hyperions. The Grand Final is being played outside and we hear the crowd cheering.* ARD *is watching it on a TV in the change rooms.* CINDY *enters.*

CINDY: How much did you put on the footy tab?
ARD: Too much.
CINDY: We. Will. Win.
   They watch the screen.
Pass it Gazza. Pass it to Kollam.
ARD: Ooof. You're right. What Gazza should have done is stayed in the trio shape with Kollam and Macca. If he played that seventy percent

of the field properly he would have dummied to the forwards that were on either side of him and then passed the ball on to the half and then the full back. There were only three defenders on the long side. Missed opportunity.

CINDY: You should be out there playing. You might not have the brawn but you've got the brains.

ARD: Who knows what the future holds?

CINDY: I'm proud of you my love. You've bent and shaped them through all of their injuries this year darling. You're my silent achiever.

> CINDY *kisses* ARD *on the forehead. The mood suddenly changes in the room as we hear the crowd outside boo. The referee whistle can be heard.*

ARD & CINDY: Gazza!

ARD: He's limping.

CINDY: His leg. No!

ARD: C'mon ref!

CINDY: We need to get him back out there! We can't play without him!

> CINDY *runs out of the change room.* KEERAN *enters with a walking stick, frail.*

KEERAN: Ard?

ARD: This is a private area.

KEERAN: If I could just speak to you for a moment.

ARD: Do I need to call security?

KEERAN: Ard. It's me. Dad.

Pause.

ARD: What do you want? Money?

KEERAN: No.

ARD: It's Kollam's grand final. Do you really think that now's the right time to show up?

KEERAN: I've been writing to you both for years.

ARD: Don't lie.

KEERAN: I understand you're angry—I would be too—

ARD: We don't wanna know you. We don't need you—we—you need to get out of here. I won't let you see Mum. No fucking way.

KEERAN: I need to speak to you all.

ARD: Get out of here now! Now!
KEERAN: Please, son—
ARD: Don't you call me your son! I am not your son!
KEERAN: *Ente mone, ninne njaan snehikkunnu. Njan nine kaanaan veendum veendum varum. Ente makane manasilavannathu vare. Veendum veendum. Njan irupathanju varshakkalam ottakku jeevichu mone. Enthe hrudayam, Ninte ammayallathe njan mattarumayum panku vachilla. Njan prarthikkam. Nee swargatilu ethum. Njanippol ethiyathu pole. Njan swargam kandethi kazhinjirikkunnu. Enikkini marikkam. Pakshe njanente jeevitham muzhuvan paazhaakki. Neeyum athe thettu aavarthikkan njaan samadhikkilla. Ninne njaan snehikkunnu mone. Ninne njaan veendum veendum kaanan varum. Monn ne manasilakkunnathu vare.* (I love you, my son. I will visit you. Again and Again. Until you understand, my son. Again and again! I have lived alone for twenty five years, my son. I have not shared myself with a single soul since your mother. I pray you will reach utopia. Like I have now. I have found utopia. I can die now. But I've wasted my whole life! I won't let you make the same mistake. I love you, my son. I will visit you again and again. Until you understand, my son.)

    ARD *pushes* KEERAN *out of the change room as* CINDY *enters through a private entrance.*

CINDY: Ard—you need to fix Gazza's leg. The ref won't hold the game. We need to get him back out there immediately!

    GAZZA *bursts in.*

GAZZA: My leg. My leg! Ard! Help me.
ARD: Where's the pain?
GAZZA: In my hammie. Owwwwww!

    CINDY *helps* GAZZA *take his shorts off revealing a sports g-string.*

CINDY: Get on the massage table Garry.
GAZZA: I need to get back out there.
ARD: Mum—go get some ice.

    CINDY *exits.*

I need you to lie down for me Gazza. I need you to stay still so I can look at your g-string. Hamstring.

SCENE NINETEEN

YOUNG MAN *and* YOUNG ANAND *stand, separated by iron bars. A male Indian* GUARD *in a prison outfit stands nearby, watching them.* YOUNG MAN *speaks to* YOUNG ANAND *in Malayalam.*

YOUNG MAN: *Anand. Dayavayi karayalle nee.* (Anand. Please don't cry.)
YOUNG ANAND: *Ithu velichennayanu.* (It's the coconut oil.)
POLICE GUARD: *Mindaradde!* (Quiet!)
   They switch to English.
YOUNG MAN: This bloody gaol was built by the British. These bloody laws were made by the British!
YOUNG ANAND: Things will change. They have to.
YOUNG MAN: I should be in there with you.
YOUNG ANAND: You bore the brunt of it last time. It's my turn.
YOUNG MAN: I've paid the bail money.
YOUNG ANAND: With what?
   YOUNG MAN *is silent.*
I don't want her money!
YOUNG MAN: It's not just her money anymore. It's our money.
YOUNG ANAND: She's been here for two months and you now have a joint bank account?
YOUNG MAN: She's pregnant Anand.
   YOUNG ANAND *begins to cry.*
YOUNG ANAND: I can't run this theatre without you Keeravani.
YOUNG MAN: Of course you can Anand. You don't need me. There are hundreds of other students.
YOUNG ANAND: You're irreplaceable.
YOUNG MAN: Marry Master-ji's daughter. She's been lost since he passed. The two of you will run the theatre perfectly.
YOUNG ANAND: Keeravani, we've been in each other's arms since we were children. You were my first kiss, my first dance partner, my first room mate, my first … love. My only love.

YOUNG MAN: I'm sorry Anand.

YOUNG ANAND: We're cursed, aren't we Keeravani? This is a curse.

YOUNG MAN: It's not a curse. We can cure ourselves.

YOUNG ANAND: How?

Pause.

Please stay with me, Keeravani?

YOUNG MAN: How could we make this work Anand? Your family would never accept me.

YOUNG ANAND: I don't care if you're from a lower caste. I don't care what my family thinks. I can't be with anyone else but you. Let's move to Bombay or Delhi no? There are others like us there.

YOUNG MAN: I'm going to Australia, Anand. I want to go to Australia.

YOUNG ANAND: She has no right to waltz in here with her pom poms and pasty white skin.

YOUNG MAN: Goodbye Anand.

YOUNG ANAND: You have a gift from the gods Keeravani. No-one can dance like you. When has any theatre company in India allowed a lower caste person to join them at such a young age? Your dancing has allowed you to transcend the dark side of Hinduism.

YOUNG MAN: Fuck the caste system.

YOUNG ANAND: Fuck it all. Dance has freed you, Keeravani. You must honour your gift. How will you dance in Australia?

YOUNG MAN: I'll start a Kathakali school in Sydney. I'll name it after you.

YOUNG ANAND: You remember what my name means?

YOUNG MAN: Of course I do.

YOUNG ANAND: What does it mean?

YOUNG MAN: Bliss.

YOUNG ANAND: I hope you find your bliss, Keeravani.

YOUNG MAN *throws himself at* ANAND *and they both hug through the bars. They kiss.*

POLICE GUARD: *Cumbikkunnat nirtuka!* (Stop kissing!)

YOUNG MAN *and* YOUNG ANAND *hold pinky fingers.*

SCENE TWENTY

BOYD *speaks to a small, gathered audience. He holds a blade and chalice.* LIRAZ *holds* KEERAN*'s urn.*

BOYD: As the sword is to the grail, the blade is to the chalice. We call upon the goddess and god and feel their love.

> BOYD *places the blade inside the chalice and moves it in and out three times.*

Let's bring our awareness back to the present now—accepting that this is where we are right now. This is who we are right now. This is where our bodies are at right now. Doesn't mean that we'll be this way tomorrow or next year … but now … this is how we are connected.

LIRAZ: And remember this is where'll we'll be operating from now on—at Shakthi Spa. Flyers are at the entrance with the change of venue and the re-branding. I designed the new logo myself.

BOYD: Thank you Liraz. We are Keeravani's chosen family. His ashes will be scattered inside this circle of love and trust. Keeravani's son will now perform his father's favourite dance.

> ARD *appears in an ornate Kathakali dress.*
>
> *Music is heard—drums and cymbals.* ARD *begins to dance a wordless piece of theatre, evoking the power of Ardha-narishvara.*
>
> *With the rising tension of the song,* ARD *dances more and more intensely—sweating, writhing, his face twitching with the evocation of shifting rasas.*
>
> *It should be beautiful, but it isn't.* ARD *is manic, unhinged, clumsy, uncentred—he isn't in control of this dance.*
>
> *At a climax in the music,* ARD *stops and utters:*

ARD: Rasa seven: Sringara. Love.

> *White light shoots all over the audience for a moment.*
>
> *Suddenly* ARD *starts to have a fit. He falls to the ground, shaking violently.*

BOYD: We should call an ambulance.

LIRAZ: No. Let him have the fit. No more medicating. Let him feel it. Let him lose control.

BOYD and LIRAZ silently watch ARD thrash and seizure on the ground, and slowly they fade away as the world around ARD folds into darkness.

Slowly, ARD's fit subsides. His limbs relax, and he stands—shakily. From the dark, ARDHA-NARISH-VARA / KEERAN appears, wiping the coloured make-up off their / his face.

ARD: Dad?

KEERAN removes the skirt, the jacket and finally his head piece.

Then, KEERAN begins to dance. ARD copies him. It is not quite the traditional movements of Kathakali, but it is derived from them. A beautiful, touching, vigorous, tender, soulful dance that they perform together.

They dance closer and closer, until the movements flow like a contemporary ballet—beautiful and flowing. KEERAN is absorbed into ARD's body—they both end their dance in a beautiful embrace. And KEERAN disappears into the darkness—content.

Then, from different directions, LIRAZ and BOYD emerge wearing a chaotic jumble of Kathakali costume, dress-ups, costume jewellery, feathers and joyful queer debris ...

The three laugh in bliss, as they continue the dance—utterly unorthodox, utterly joyful.

LIRAZ cups ARD's face with her hands. They kiss.

BOYD cups LIRAZ's face with his hands. They kiss.

ARD cups BOYD's face with his hands. They kiss.

Shocked for a moment, the three pull away—then dive back in together, kissing each other wildly, their bodies intertwined, limbs and costumes entangling.

SCENE TWENTY-ONE

CINDY *stands in a white wedding dress, barking orders to terrified assistants and caterers who crisscross the stage lugging camera equipment and running cables.*

CINDY: I don't care if you've dislocated your shoulder at training, Israel. Go and find the make up artist. Run! Are the television cameras ready, Fetu? Make sure they get the Hyperions Stadium signage in the shot. Gazza for gods sake stop hanging around in the mens change room and go and remind Waylon that we'll only enter to verse one and the chorus of the Tina Turner song now. Verse two is cut. And make sure he walks to the beat of the music this time. I need my make up checked! Israel?! Fuck. Fuck. Fuck. Trish! Make sure the Crucifit group are not seated in front of the cameras—they're all fatties and if they stand up they'll block the view.

    ARD *enters.*

What are you doing here? I'm about to walk down the field. Where's Kollam!? He's never here when you need him.
ARD: I've come to walk you down the field, Mum.
CINDY: You didn't RSVP.
ARD: I thought it was insensitive of you to write 'To Ard and Partner.'
CINDY: You're lucky I invited you at all after the way you've ignored me.
ARD: I needed time to work things out.
CINDY: Well now's not the time for any surprises. I'm about to get married.
ARD: Is it okay for me to be here?
CINDY: Of course it is—you're my son. But just lay low okay? Everyone in the club knows what happened and why you left. I knew you'd end up like your father.
ARD: I'd be proud to be like dad.
CINDY: So you are ... gay?
ARD: I'd be lying to you if I said I was and the last thing this family needs is more lies.
CINDY: Look—I don't care if you're gay, okay? Just don't tell anyone at the club. I'm not going to disown you for being like your father. Alright? Hug?

ARD *won't hug her.*

If you've got a boyfriend that's fine. Bring him to the reception then. I'll deal with the boofheads. We'll just say he's your mate from the gym.

ARD: Is it only plus one?

CINDY: What?

ARD*'s facial muscles move up and down into the Kathakali facial expression of Viram. Rainbow lighting shoots around the stage for a moment.*

ARD: Rasa eight: Viram. Heroic.

ARD *takes a deep breath.*

Can we add an 's' on the invitation? To Ard and partners.

CINDY: No comprehende.

ARD: I'd like to bring a girl and a boy to your wedding. Liraz and another man.

CINDY: For godsake. Choose which way you're inclined before we're all the laughing stock of the League.

ARD: It's not a choice, Mum.

CINDY: Of course it's a choice.

ARD: I don't know how to describe how I feel ... but it feels beautiful. I'd like you to meet him.

CINDY: So you're ... bisexual?

ARD: I thought that I was at first but—

CINDY: There's no such thing as bisexuality. You're either straight or gay. Which one is it?

ARD: Mum. I'm in a relationship with a guy and a girl. The three of us are in a relationship.

CINDY: Polyamory?

ARD: I'm not needing to define what it is but whatever it is—it works.

CINDY: You're joking right? I can't believe my ears. You've been brainwashed. Again and again! Indoctrinated.

ARD: Not at all. Everything feels expansive. I'd like you to meet Boyd properly.

CINDY: Who's Boyd?

ARD: One of my partners. You've already met him actually. He was dad's ... nurse.

CINDY *laughs hysterically.*
Everyone's a little pansexual.
CINDY: Pansexual?! What's that? The term for getting frisky when your gold panning?
ARD: Pansexuals fall in love with the person inside. With people—not just with their sex or gender identity.
CINDY: Oh Christ. Soon three people will want to get married. Four!
ARD: I truly hoped that you wouldn't react like this. What happened to the adventurous young woman that went to India when she was young? What happened to the woman who fell for a man who dressed as a woman?
CINDY: She grew up. She learnt about the world. She wanted to succeed and she's a CEO and chairman now. You should do the same.
ARD: May I bring Boyd and Liraz to your reception? As my partners?
CINDY: If you bring your polly gold-panning sex friends to my wedding—I'll never talk to you again.
ARD: They're not sex friends. They're my lovers. My loves. I love both of them, Mum.
CINDY: India fucked you up.
ARD: You fucked me up.
CINDY: Don't embarrass me again Ard. Do not. This is my big day. Don't make this all about you.
ARD: I'm not. I'd like to come to my mother's wedding with my partners.
CINDY: *Woman's Day* photographers are here! They're doing a live broadcast on *The Footy Show*. Do you want all of this in the tabloids? To shame your brother? Where the fuck is Kollam?!
ARD: Mum, I'm happy.
CINDY: You're sick.
ARD: The fits have stopped. Since falling in love with Liraz and Boyd—they've stopped.
CINDY: I want my son back
ARD: Mum, please let Boyd and Liraz come. They're outside waiting.
CINDY: You've gone mad. You've joined some sort of cult, haven't you? Just like your father. I thought when he moved here he'd be less religious but it amped up even more. He started wearing gemstones. Chanting all sorts of things to different gods. Calling upon deities when dancing with you. It was too much. He was buying bulk honey

ACT TWO

from Campbells Cash and Carry to offer to the deities he prayed to. He'd leave fruit out for them. Yoghurt. Flowers. We got ants in the house and fruit flies everywhere—and let me tell you—not even Mortein can kill those little fuckers. It was too much. I don't mind a bit of incense and Enya but honey? Everything just got sticky. Fanaticism is something I just don't support.

We hear Kollam chanting the Hyperions Footy chant. A crowd call out madly and join in.

KOLLAM: [*off*] Hyperions are on the run!
CINDY, KOLLAM & CROWD: We're on our way to win the scrum! Oy! Oy! Oy oy!
KOLLAM: [*off*] Happy wedding Mum! Cheers! Up ya bum!

We hear Tina Turner's 'Simply the Best' over the loud speaker.

CINDY: I'm on. I'll walk down the field on my own. We're all solo on this earth, Ard. We walk alone. And no partnership whether it be a pair or a trio can change that.
ARD: Why did you write to Ard and partner on my invitation then?
CINDY: Because it's etiquette. It's tradition.
ARD: I'm done with tradition.

ARD *exits.*

CINDY *is forlorn for a private moment then attempts to steel herself. Gathering her bouquet, she steps out onto the footy field— to the roar of a crowd and a thousand flashing phone cameras. Waving, she walks down the footy field towards* WAYLON—*who stands itching the neck of his tuxedo uncomfortably.*

WAYLON *turns to face* CINDY—*and,* CINDY *gasps. Suddenly, his face has been replaced by* KEERAN*'s.*

CINDY: Keeravani.

KEERAN *turns to the audience. His eyes widen and his face moves into the Kathakali dance facial expression of Santam. Black light surrounds him for a moment.*

KEERAN: Rasa nine: My favourite. Santam. Peace.

KEERAN *turns back towards* CINDY, *and once again—to her relief—she sees* WAYLON *staring back at her aghast expression with confusion.* CINDY *collects herself and turns to a microphone, addressing the crowd and the video cameras.*

CINDY: Thank you for being here tonight.

CINDY*'s dress begins to blow in the breeze with the sound of bells and distant drums.*

There's been a large void inside of me for many years and Waylon has filled that hole with so much substance. Waylon, you give me access to so much ... expandable, inter-dimensional, gold pannable, pure ... Christian love. I am ... porous for you. Holy. This club is my church. This sport is my religion. With that in mind, Waylon and I would like for us all to pray. Together.

A large gust of wind blows into the stadium.

In the name of the father, the son and the holy spirit ...

A large peacock feather suddenly blows on stage. Immediately captivated by it, CINDY *falls silent. Cameras continue to flash. In the growing silence, the crowd begins to shift and murmur.* CINDY *steps towards the peacock feather, hypnotized, dragging the train of her wedding dress behind her. She bends down, and picks it up ...*

*And the moment she stands—*CINDY *finds herself in a grove. There is the sound of cicadas, deafeningly loud ... And somewhere, nearby, through the foliage—the sound of people making love.*

CINDY *walks towards the sound of the lovers, but in another gust of wind,* CINDY*'s enormous wedding dress catches and flips inside out—revealing a magnificent blue-and-green peacock plumage.*

The plumage-dress blows in the wind, shielding CINDY*'s view. She struggles against it, attempting to push it down—but it is too big and all encompassing.*

Suddenly, KEERAN *appears again. He places a lighter in* CINDY*'s hand. He keeps a grip over her hand, and together they ignite the lighter and hold it up to the plumage-dress.*

In an instant, the dress burns away—releasing the loud, shrill squawk of an angry peacock ... And on the other side is revealed:

ARD, LIRAZ, and BOYD. *They are locked together, naked, in a glowing tableau of ecstasy and love.*

CINDY's *eyes fill with tears—it's a beautiful sight for her to behold. She squeezes* KEERAN's *hand.*

So mote it be.

THE END

GRIFFIN THEATRE COMPANY IN ASSOCIATION WITH
SYDNEY WORLDPRIDE 2023 PRESENTS

SEX MAGICK

BY NICHOLAS BROWN

17 FEBRUARY – 25 MARCH 2023 | SBW STABLES THEATRE

CAST & CREATIVES

Playwright & Co-Director
Nicholas Brown

Dramaturg & Co-Director
Declan Greene

Choreographer
Raghav Handa

Set & Costumer Designer
Mason Browne

Lighting Designer
Kelsey Lee

Composer & Sound Designer
Danni A. Esposito

Video Designer
Solomon Thomas

Associate Cultural Dramaturg
Jay Emmanuel

Community Engagement Director
Gary Paramanathan

Intimacy Coordinator
Chloe Dallimore

Malayalam Translation
Anish Chacko, Athira Pradeep, Rashmi Ravindran

Production Associate
Emma Van Veen

Production Manager
Saint Clair

Voice & Accent Coach
Nikki Zhao

Stage Manager
Isabella Kerdijk

With
Blazey Best, Raj Labade, Stephen Madsen, Veshnu Narayanasamy, Mansoor Noor, Catherine Văn-Davies

---

Griffin acknowledges the generosity of the Seaborn, Broughton & Walford Foundation in allowing it the use of the SBW Stables Theatre rent free, less outgoings, since 1986.

PLAYWRIGHT'S NOTE

Sex Magick is a queer anarchic romp that merges the ancient South Indian art of Kathakali with modern storytelling. It follows the journey of its protagonist Ard Panicker as he subconsciously tries to shed his conditioning in order to reach queer utopia.

I first started writing this story way back in 2009 when I was living in India and heading home to Sydney for short visits. In Sydney I was dating a massage therapist (white) who was about to become a tantric practitioner. I was initially confronted by this revelation, then jealous, then angry with myself for not being open-minded enough at the time to date someone in this field. I was assured that the job expansion was for health and spiritual purposes only. I was eventually roped into being the voice of the online tantric course that was part of their new business plan—guiding couples towards sexual ecstasy. The business didn't last—but my interest in this area remained. Why was I initially confronted? Was I ashamed? What was I ashamed of? Why do we often separate sex, health and spirituality? Was I annoyed that my white mate was appropriating Indian spirituality? Then I began to wonder—what if an audience was confronted with the same issues? After reading many books by queer Indian mythologist **Devdutt Pattnaik** (brown guy) and several essays by the American Indologist **Wendy Doniger** (white lady), I began to wonder—should myth be for everyone or just for the people from its country of origin? Should wellness techniques be for everyone or just for the people from its country of origin? I believe that myth and wellness should be for everyone.

I further developed this story when heading back to India where I found myself playing aggressive villains in Bollywood. Being mixed race, I've always been interested in the grey area between cultures, and the feeling of being 'half'. In a bid to fully explore my South Asian heritage, I became quite obsessed with the violent, demonic and magical world of Indian mythology. And in the process, I became intrigued by the vast differences between western and eastern masculinity; specifically, the fluidity of gender in Indian myths.

Whilst living in India, I also found it intriguing that so many Indians wanted to be American. Conversely, when moving to Los Angeles I found it curious that so many people were in touch with Indian culture and yoga. More people said 'namaste' to me in Los Angeles than they ever did in Mumbai. I found the differences in masculinity between east and west so compelling that I began looking into other religions and ideologies; discovering similarities between Indian mythology, ancient Greek mythology, Hinduism and even modern witchcraft. It became clear to me that I had to create a magic(k)al story about a brown man finding himself through sex, spirituality and mythology.

The story was initially a film script I wrote called *Tantra 2* (as in Tantra squared—to the power of two) that developed into a play in 2017 thanks to Playwriting Australia/Australian Plays Transform. Annoyed when people kept asking about *Tantra 1* (lol), I changed the title to *Sex Magick* and it stuck. Magick with a 'k' because magick is described (by **Anthony Crowley**—occultist—white) as anything that moves a person closer to fulfilling their destiny.

And so it was my destiny that **Declan Greene** was brave enough to see my vision and develop the script with me. He's been working as a dramaturg/director on the project since 2020 and I can honestly say—it's been an absolute joy. I was a huge fan of his work having seen several of his **Sisters Grimm** shows and will forever be grateful that I've had the chance to collaborate with him. He's helped whip the script into a shape that I'm extremely proud of and assisted me in distilling my vision with razor-sharp focus. The whole process with Declan and Griffin has indeed been magick.

As suggested by the title, 'sex' plays a big part in this story. But it's important to note that the sexual aspects of this play haven't been created for sensationalism. They're tied to something deeper, something spiritual, something healing and life-affirming. Rather than seeing these moments as smutty, my hope is that audiences will find them incredibly moving, and beautiful.

It's no secret that in India you have to exercise discretion when being sexual. It's frowned upon for people of the opposite sex to hold hands in public and sex before marriage is taboo. Whilst living there I became confused by the hypocrisy of such virtuous morality coming from the country that gave us the *Kama Sutra* and realised these attitudes are the result of lingering British colonialism, which affects Indian legislation to this day. Being Anglo-Indian myself and having a lineage from British Indian colonialism, I realised that I was the perfect person to explore this fascinating paradox. I was always sceptical of the idea of 'god' being a man, and in India I embraced the ideology that 'the ultimate universal power' perhaps comes from the balance between male and female, the goddess and the god—Shiva and Shakthi. This balance is essentially what *Sex Magick* is about—harmony and balance between male and female energy through tantra.

Like Kathakali theatre, *Sex Magick* is divided into nine chapters (rasas). These rasas cover a range of human emotions including love, anger, sorrow, laughter, courage, terror and wonder. The play also uses colour to explore the seven chakras of the human body; energy centres that hold our egos, our ability to connect with ourselves, each other and higher realms (if you're into that kind of thing). I am and I hope audiences will be too after seeing this play.

Above all, I hope that *Sex Magick* will open minds, hearts and dissipate any shame that we feel in regards to sex, our bodies and our gender.

Nicholas Brown
He/Him/His
Playwright

BIOGRAPHIES

NICHOLAS BROWN
PLAYWRIGHT & CO-DIRECTOR

Since graduating from NIDA, Nicholas has forged an international career across film, television and theatre as an actor, singer, writer and Bollywood leading man. Nicholas' previous credits as a playwright include: for Griffin: *Lighten Up*; and for National Theatre of Parramatta/Sydney for National Theatre of Parramatta/Sydney Festival/True West: Lost in Books *(Myths and Legends)*. Some of his recent theatre credits as an actor include: for Belvoir: *Counting and Cracking*; for New Theatricals: *Come From Away*; for Queensland Theatre: *Bernhardt/Hamlet*, *Taming of the Shrew*; and for Sydney Theatre Company: *The Long Forgotten Dream*, *Still Point Turning*. His television credits as a writer include: for ABC: *Playschool*, *Unlisted*, *The Wonder Gang*. His television credits as an actor include: for ABC: *The Code*, *The Elegant Gentlemen's Guide to Knife Fighting*, *Harrow*, *In Our Blood*, *The Letdown*, *Play School*, *The PM's Daughter*, *Wakefield*; for Foxtel: *Upright*; for Network 10: *The Cooks*, *Mr. & Mrs. Murder*, *White Collar Blue*; for Nine Network: *Amazing Grace*, *After the Verdict*, *Underbelly: The Man Who Got Away;* for Peacock: *Joe Vs Carole*; and for Seven Network: *City Homicide*, *Home & Away*, *Packed to the Rafters*. His film credits include: *Christmas on the Farm*, *Dance Academy*, *Kites*, *Laka*, *Love You To Death*, *A Man's Gotta Do*, *A Perfect Pairing*, *Pratichhaya*, *Random 8*, *Sedition*, *Temptation*, *Unindian*. Nicholas has also been the lead singer for, written and recorded with several bands including The Modernists and Luck Now.

DECLAN GREENE
DRAMATURG & CO-DIRECTOR

Declan is the Artistic Director of Griffin Theatre Company and works as a playwright, dramaturg and director. As a director, his credits include: for Griffin: *Dogged*, *Green Park*, *Whitefella Yella Tree*; for Malthouse Theatre: *Wake in Fright*; for Malthouse Theatre and Sydney Theatre Company: *Blackie Blackie Brown*; for Sydney Theatre Company: *Hamlet: Prince of Skidmark*; for ZLMD Shakespeare Company: *Conviction*. As a playwright, his work includes *Eight Gigabytes of Hardcore Pornography*, *The Homosexuals, or 'Faggots'*, *Melancholia*, *Moth*, and *Pompeii L.A.* Declan co-founded queer experimental theatre company Sisters Grimm with Ash Flanders in 2006, and has directed and co-created all their productions to date, including: for Griffin Independent and Theatre Works: *Summertime in the Garden of Eden*; for Malthouse Theatre and Sydney Theatre Company: *Calpurnia Descending*; for Melbourne Theatre Company: *Lilith: The Jungle Girl*; and for Sydney Theatre Company: *Little Mercy*. He was previously Resident Artist at Malthouse Theatre.

RAGHAV HANDA
CHOREOGRAPHER

Trained in contemporary dance, Raghav Handa draws on the principles of Indian kathak to create multifaceted, engaging explorations of modern Australian identity. Raghav has worked with some of Australia's most renowned choreographers and companies including Contemporary Asian Australian Performance, Force Majeure, Martin Del Amo, Marylin Miller, The National Theatre of Parramatta, Sue Healey, Sydney Dance Company and Vicki Van Hout. His works have been presented across Australia and internationally, including *Double Delicious* for CAAP (Sydney Festival season and National Tour), and at Adelaide OzAsia, AsiaTOPA, Attakkalari Dance Company (India), Dancehouse, Darwin Festival, Dunedin Festival (New Zealand), Keir Choreographic Awards, Performance Space's Liveworks Festival, Rich Mix London, and for Sydney Opera House's Unwrapped season. Raghav's works challenge cultural and contemporary norms by navigating the 'preciousness' and complexities that surround traditional hierarchies and by utilising his Indian heritage to create spaces that foster robust discussion and risk taking—he encourages his audience to come to their own conclusions rather than imposing his own. His creations are novel, engaging and often playful—but he also likes to play with fire!

MASON BROWNE
SET & COSTUME DESIGNER

Mason is a descendant of the Darug people and an award-winning creative director, designer and producer working across theatre, film, television, and live events. His theatre credits as designer include: for Griffin: *Whitefella Yella Tree*; for ATYP: *The Deb*; for Critical Stages: *Nosferatu*; for Dancing Giant Productions: *Eternityland*; for Hayes Theatre Co: *American Psycho*, for which he won a Sydney Theatre Award for Best Costume Design of an Independent Production, *Jekyll & Hyde*, *Cry-Baby*, *Darlinghurst Nights*, *Young Frankenstein*; for Neil Gooding Productions: *Leap*; for New Theatre: *Summer Rain*; for Railway Street Theatre Company: *Sunday in the Park with George*; for Seymour Centre: *The Importance of Being Earnest*; for Tantrum Theatre: *Powerforce Live*, *Riot!*, *Savage Naked Love*; and for The Theatre Division: *Ruthless!*. His television credits include: for Endemol Shine: *Big Brother* and *Ready Steady Cook*. His film credits include: for Sydney Festival: *The Human Voice*. Mason has produced, designed and directed events across Australia and the USA with clients including Audi, Beyond the Valley and Lost Paradise Music Festivals, Darlinghurst Theatre Company, Mercedes-Benz Fashion Week Australia, Netflix, Opera Australia, Stereosonic, Sydney Dance Company, Vodka O and Woodford Folk Festival. He is the Co-Founder of Gaytimes, Australia's premier LGBTIQ Music Festival and Creative Producer at Dark Mofo in nipaluna / Hobart. With an eye for style details, Mason honed his skill as a creative director and stylist on music videos and fashion editorial, including for Abby Dobson, Dappled Cities Fly, Lisa Mitchell, Marcia Hines and Red Riders, as well as the publications Culture, InStyle, Oyster, The Vine, Vogue Brides Australia and Yen. Mason holds a Bachelor of Dramatic Art in Design from NIDA.

KELSEY LEE
LIGHTING DESIGNER

Kelsey is a lighting, set and costume designer for theatre and film. Her theatre credits as a lighting designer include: for Griffin: *Whitefella Yella Tree*; for Griffin Lookout: *A is for Apple*; for Bell Shakespeare: *The Comedy of Errors*; for Belvoir: *A Room of One's Own*; for Belvoir 25A: *Extinction of the Learned Response*, *Kasama Kita*, *Skyduck*; for Darlinghurst Theatre Company: *I'm With Her*; for Ensemble Theatre: *A Letter for Molly*, *Killing Katie: Confessions Of A Bookclub*, *Outdated*, *Unqualified 2: Still Unqualified*; for Green Door/KXT: *Good Dog*, *If We Got Some More Cocaine I Could Show You How I Love You*; for Outhouse/KXT: *Trevor*; for National Theatre of Parramatta/Sydney Festival: *Queen Fatima*; for Red Line Productions at the Old Fitz: *Fierce*, *The Humans*; and as Associate Lighting Designer: for Belvoir: *At What Cost?*; *Blue*. Her credits as set, costume and lighting designer include: for Griffin Lookout: *Jali*; for Australian Chamber Orchestra: *There's a Sea in My Bedroom*, *Wilfred Gordon McDonald Partridge*; for Belvoir 25A: *Destroy, She Said*; for NIDA: *LULU: A Modern Sex Tragedy*. Kelsey designed the set for Hayes Theatre Co's *Catch Me If You Can* and was Co-Designer for Griffin's *Shabbat Dinner*. Her film credits include Production Assistant on *Long Story Short* (See Pictures) and she was in the Set Dec Department for *Shang Chi and The Legend of the 10 Rings* (Marvel).

DANNI A. ESPOSITO
COMPOSER & SOUND DESIGNER

Danni is a non-binary composer and sound designer from Naarm, working across theatre and film. They are a recent graduate of Victorian College of the Arts and hold a Bachelor of Fine Arts in Production. Danni's credits include: as composer and sound designer: for Bighouse Arts: *Tram Lights Up*; for The Burrow: *Slut*; for Darebin Arts: *Hydra*; for Darlinghurst Theatre Company: *Overflow*; for Essential Theatre: *The Dream Laboratory*; for Fever103 Theatre: *Treats*; for La Mama: *Cactus*; for Malthouse Theatre/Darlinghurst Theatre Company: *Stay Woke*; for Midsumma Festival: *Adam*, *Guerilla Sabbath*, *Slutnik*; for Melbourne Writers Festival: *Never Said Motel*; for New Theatricals: *Darkness*; for Patalog Theatre: *Punk Rock*; for Red Stitch: *Fast Food*; for Three Fates Theatre Company: *Land*. Their credits as sound designer include: for Melbourne Theatre Company: *The Sound Inside*; and as assistant sound designer: for Melbourne Theatre Company: *Sunday*. Danni was a panel member for the 2022 Green Room Awards. Danni received a Green Room Award nomination for their work on *Hydra*. They are currently nominated for a Sydney Theatre Award for Best Composer for their work on *Overflow*.

SOLOMON THOMAS
VIDEO DESIGNER

Solomon Thomas is a theatre maker and video artist. His work explores the intersection between the physical and digital in theatre, experimenting with how theatre and film can co-exist in a live context. He works as a director, performer, puppeteer, and video designer and is driven by how these practices meet formally. His recent theatre credits include: for Brand X: *The Sucker*; for Sydney Opera House: *What the Ocean Said*. Solomon is a core member of re:group performance collective, whose work *Coil* was presented at the Opera House, Mona Foma, PACT and Next Wave. Solomon has also worked with Branch Nebula, My Darling Patricia, Nick Cave, Applespiel, Studio A, Chiara Guidi, and Erth. Solomon is currently Artistic Associate with Erth Visual & Physical Inc (2014–22) and has toured with them throughout the UK, UAE, Hong Kong, Singapore, Australia and Japan.

JAY EMMANUEL
ASSOCIATE CULTURAL DRAMATURG

Born in India and based in Australia, Jay is an internationally-acclaimed theatremaker, director, festival programmer, and is currently the Artistic Director of Encounter Theatre company based in Perth. His credits as a performer include: for Belvoir: *Counting and Cracking*; for Radhouane El-Meddeb: *Heroes Prelude*. Jay's recent credits as a playwright/librettist and director include *Children of the Sea* for Encounter Theatre; he is currently commissioned to adapt the play into a libretto by WASO to premiere in April 2023. Jay is a core deviser and performer in Why Not's epic production of *MAHABHARATA* premiering at Shaw Festival (Canada) and the Barbican (UK) in 2023. In addition, he has also worked in the programming team at OzAsia festival (Adelaide) and St George's Dance and Theatre (Perth). Jay is currently a lead creative with Performing Lines WA and was part of Belvoir's Artists at Work Program; he is an alumnus of the prestigious Australia Council Future Leaders Program.

GARY PARAMANATHAN
COMMUNITY ENGAGEMENT DIRECTOR

Gary Paramanathan works at the intersection of arts, culture and community. Born in Sri Lanka and raised in Australia, Gary studied arts management, screen and communications. While his day-to-day job is arts administration, he has written and directed a number of short films, including for ABC iView. He has written feature essays and recounted personal narratives, including for The Guardian. Gary also runs a live storytelling night focusing on PoC stories, called *Them Heavy People*. He currently focuses on writing and performing short works of autobiography and fiction. He was shortlisted for the Deborah Cass Prize in 2021, won a Writing NSW mentorship and is soon to be published in a Sweatshop anthology. Gary is passionate about migrant and diaspora storytelling and hopes to add to the rich tapestry of diverse Australian storytelling through his work.

BALI PADDA
CREATIVE PRODUCER

Bali Padda is a multidisciplinary director, actor, producer, developer/dramaturg and screen executive across both stage and screen. His directing credits include: for National Theatre of Parramatta: *Guards at the Taj*; for Sydney WorldPride 2023 and Mardi Gras (2017): *Sunderella*. His producing credits include: for Griffin Lookout: *Lighten Up*; for Mardi Gras: *In the Space Between, Sunderella*; for MEAA: *Equity 75: A Toast to Equity*; for Oz Showbiz Cares/Equity Fights AIDS: *Hats Off!*; and for Pearly Productions (online): *Minority Box*. Bali also works creatively with a number of screen funding agencies as a story developer and development assessor, as well as in the theatre sector in creative development and dramaturgy. Outside of creative arts work, he has a track record in strategy, leadership and development of the screen and arts sectors through roles at Screen Australia, Create NSW and elected positions at MEAA as a Federal Councillor and founding Chair of the Equity Diversity Committee.

CHLOË DALLIMORE
INTIMACY COORDINATOR

Chloë is internationally trained and accredited as an Intimacy Coordinator by Ita O'Brien of Intimacy on Set (UK). Recent credits for the stage include: for Belvoir: *Counting and Cracking*; for Red Line Productions at the Sydney Opera House: *Amadeus*; and for Sydney Theatre Company: *A Raisin in the Sun, The Tempest*. Chloë's television credits include: for Netflix: *Heartbreak High, Pieces of Her*; and her film credits include George Miller's *Three Thousand Years of Longing* and Benjamin Millepied's *Carmen*. With a life-long journey in professional dance, and as an award-winning musical theatre performer, Chloë's career has seen her work as a Resident/Associate Choreographer on mainstage productions such as *Billy Elliot, Oliver!* and *Annie*, as well as perform lead roles in productions such as *The Addams Family, Chicago, The Producers* and *Thoroughly Modern Millie*. Chloë is honoured to work for the first time with Griffin team!

NIKKI ZHAO
VOICE AND ACCENT COACH

Yuanlei (Nikki) Zhao is a voice and dialect coach and teaching artist based in Naarm/Melbourne. Originally from Shanghai, Nikki is a bilingual coach, Lessac practitioner, a recipient of the Creative Victoria's Creative Learning Partnerships grant and is a tutor at VCA. Nikki has worked as dialect coach on productions including: for Creative Learning Victoria: *Abbotsford DNA Through Time*; for Intercultural Theatre Institute: *4.48 Psychosis*; for NIDA: *Goldilocks, When Vampires Shop*; *Goldilocks*; for Red Stitch: *Caught*; and for SBS: *Appetite*.

ISABELLA KERDIJK
STAGE MANAGER

Isabella graduated from the production course at the National Institute of Dramatic Art in 2008. Her previous credits as a stage manager include: for Griffin: *And No More Shall We Part*, *Green Park*, *Replay*, *The Smallest Hour*, *Ugly Mugs*, *Whitefella Yella Tree*, *Wicked Sisters*, *This Year's Ashes*; for Belvoir: *The Dog/The Cat*, *The Drover's Wife*, *An Enemy of the People*, *Every Brilliant Thing*, *Fangirls*, *Girl Asleep*, *The Glass Menagerie*, *Hir*, *Jasper Jones*, *Kill the Messenger*, *Mother*, *Mother Courage and Her Children*, *My Name is Jimi*, *Stories I Want to Tell You In Person* (National Tour), *The Sugar House*, *Thyestes* (European Tours), *Winyanboga Yurringa*; for Circus Oz: *Cranked Up*; for Darlinghurst Theatre Company: *Fourplay*, *Ride*, *Silent Night*; for Ensemble Theatre: *Boxing Day BBQ*, *Rainman*, *The Ruby Sunrise*; for Legs on the Wall: *Bubble*; for LWAA: *The Mousetrap* (Australia/New Zealand Tours); for Spiegelworld: *Empire*; for Sydney Theatre Company: *Blithe Spirit*. Isabella was a production coordinator for Opera Australia on Sydney Harbour: *Carmen* and production manager/stage manager for A-List Entertainment: *Puppetry of the Penis*. She has also worked on various festivals, including The Garden of Unearthly Delights, Sydney Festival and the Woodford Folk Festival.

BLAZEY BEST
CINDY/GONDESHWAR/ALLI-JANE

One of Australia's most versatile and accomplished actresses, Blazey has an extensive list of performing credits and was most recently seen in Red Line Productions' *Amadeus*. Her theatre credits include: for Griffin: *Dogged*, *Strange Attractor;* for Bell Shakespeare: *The Comedy of Errors* (National and UK Tours), *In a Nutshell*, *Much Ado About Nothing*, *Richard III*, *The Servant of Two Masters*, *Troilus + Cressida*, *The War of the Roses*; for Belvoir: *Death of a Salesman*, *Ivanov*, for which she won a Sydney Theatre Award for Best Actress in a Supporting Role, *Medea*, for which she won a Sydney Theatre Award for Best Actress in a Leading Role, *Miss Julie*, *My Brilliant Career*, *Nora*, *Wild Duck* (International Tours); for Luckiest Productions: *Gypsy*, *Miracle City*, for which she won a Sydney Theatre Award for Best Performance by an Actress in a Musical, *Only Heaven Knows*; for Luna Hare: *B-Girl*; for Michael Coppel: *Fawlty Towers*; for Showtune Productions: *Hedwig and the Angry Inch*; for Sydney and Adelaide Festivals: *The Iliad Out Loud*; for Sydney Theatre Company: *Summer Rain*, *Wharf Revue*, *Arcadia*, *Travesties*, *Troupers*. Blazey's previous film credits include *Powder Burn*, *Ruben Guthrie*, *Stealth*, *Ten Empty* and *West*. Her television credits include: for ABC: *Janet King*, *Rake*, *Significant Others*; Channel 7: *Between Two Worlds*, *The Killing Field*, *Home and Away*, *A Place to Call Home*; and for Netflix: *Pieces of Her*.

RAJ LABADE
ARD/YOUNG KEERAN

Raj began acting in high school performing in various musicals, plays and comedy sketches. At the age of 17, he began his professional career as Lewis in the Netflix feature film *Back of the Net*. Raj's theatre credits include: for Belvoir: *Tell Me I'm Here*; for Belvoir 25A: *Never Closer*; for Performing Lines: *Mary Stuart*. While completing his Bachelor of Fine Arts (Acting) at WAAPA, Raj was the recipient of multiple prestigious awards: the 2020 Speech and Drama Teachers Association Poetry Prize, the 2021 Vice Chancellor's Shakespeare Award and the 2021 Leslie Anderson Award for Best Graduating Actor in his final showcase performance.

STEPHEN MADSEN
MANMATHA/DRAYTON/GAZZA

Stephen's theatre credits include: for Arts Centre Melbourne in association with Showwork: *Heathers: The Musical*; for Darlinghurst Theatre Company: *Torch Song Trilogy*; for Dead Puppet Society/Legs on the Wall: *Holding Achilles*; for Hayes Theatre Company: *Rent*, *The View UpStairs*; for Red Line Productions at the Old Fitz: *Cleansed*; for Sport for Jove: *One Flew Over the Cuckoo's Nest*; Sydney Theatre Company: *Muriel's Wedding* (Original Run and National Tour), *White Pearl*; for Trevor Ashley and Phil Scott: *Moulin Scrooge*. His film credits include: *Marley, Someone*. His television credits include: for Seven Network: *Miss Fisher's Modern Murder Mysteries*, *Secret Bridesmaid's Business*. He features on the Original Cast Recording of *Muriel's Wedding*. Stephen trained at WAAPA, is a three-time Sydney Theatre Award nominee and winner of the TDP/ASCAP Bound for Broadway Scholarship.

VESHNU NARAYANASAMY
KEERAN/ARDH-ANARISH-VARA/ANAND/WAYLON

Veshnu is an established professional performing artist trained in several Asian classical dance styles and traditional martial arts. He holds a PG Dip in Dance (Distinction) and an MA in Dance (Honors) from the University of Auckland. In addition to being a full-time creative practitioner, Veshnu started his PhD research with the Faculty of Anthropology at the University of Auckland and currently continues his research with the Victoria College of Arts (VCA) in Melbourne. He has been granted a full scholarship from the Australian Commonwealth Government and the University of Melbourne for his research. A consummate dancer, Veshnu is one of very few Indian Classical dancers from Singapore to have achieved a high professional status in the art form. He has developed his kinetic skills both in the traditional genres of Bharatanatyam and Odissi, as well as in the innovative sphere of new dance vocabulary, to emerge not only as a dynamic and intelligent artist, but also as a choreographer. His Bharatanatyam and Odissi has a unique and vibrant style, which has evolved out of his perseverance in the search for artistic excellence. Having had his initial and foundation studies in Singapore, Veshnu furthered his training in India. Since 1995, he has been a principal dancer with numerous dance companies in Australia. Parallel to his development in Indian classical dance is his involvement with contemporary Western dance and experimental research projects. He has choreographed, directed and produced several full-length works for various dance companies, many of these works are a combination of multidisciplinary practices of dance, theatre and music. Veshnu has won recognition for his artistry and professionalism with the Singapore Young Artist Award and with several project grants from the National Arts Council and Arts Fund.

MANSOOR NOOR
BOYD/YOUNG ANAND/COREY

Mansoor is a graduate from the Actors Centre Australia and Griffith Film School. He has recently returned from New York where he was performing in the Off-Off Broadway show *The Culture*, produced by Powersuit Productions. His theatre credits include: for Belvoir: *Stop Girl*; for Belvoir 25A: *Son of Byblos*, *Beirut Adrenalin*; for New Theatre: *Stupid F$@king Bird*; for KXT bAKEHOUSE: *The Laden Table*, *Omar & Dawn*, *Visiting Hours*; for Monkey Baa: *Where the Streets Had a Name*; for National Theatre of Parramatta: *The Comedy of Errors*; for Q Theatre: *Daisy Moon Was Born This Way*; for Red Line Productions: *Belleville*, *Just Live!*, *Safety Switch*; and for Sydney Theatre Company: for Sydney Theatre Company: *Grand Horizons*. Mansoor's television credits include: for ABC: *Cleverman*, *The PM's Daughter*, *Rake*, *Trip for Biscuits*; for Channel 10: *The Secrets She Keeps*; for Foxtel: *Colin From Accounts*. His feature film credits include *The Furnace*, *Risen*, *Project Eden* and *Sit. Stay. Love*. His latest comedy short film, *Why Not Both*, will be playing at this year's Sydney Mardi Gras Film Festival.

CATHERINE VĂN-DAVIES
LIRAZ/YOUNG CINDY/JOJO

Catherine Văn-Davies is a multi-award-winning Vietnamese-Australian stage and screen actor based in Sydney. Her theatre credits include: for Griffin: *The Turquoise Elephant*; for Apocalypse Theatre Company: *Angels in America*, for which she won the 2020 Sydney Theatre Award for Best Supporting Actor; for Arthur: *Cut Snake, Superhero Training Academy, The Myth Project: Twin, Waltzing Woolloomooloo: The Tale of Frankie Jones*; for Bell Shakespeare: *The Merchant of Venice, The Misanthrope, Titus Andronicus*; for Belvoir: *An Enemy of the People, Back at the Dojo, The Kiss*; for Chunky Move with Falk Richter: *Complexity of Belonging*; for Little Ones Theatre: *Dangerous Liaisons, Dracula, Dangerous Liaisons*; for MKA: *sex. violence. blood. gore.*; for Sydney Theatre Company: *Playing Beatie Bow, No Pay? No Way!*; for Sydney Theatre Company/National Theatre of Parramatta: *White Pearl*, for which she received the 2020 Sydney Theatre Award for Best Ensemble; and for Sydney Theatre Company/Malthouse Theatre: *Going Down*. Her screen credits include: for ABC: *Barons, The Letdown*; for Black Pills: *Pet Killer*; for Foxtel: *Fighting Season, The Twelve*; for Nine Network: *Amazing Grace*; for Photoplay Films: *It's Fine I'm Fine*; and for SBS: *Hungry Ghosts*. Catherine graduated from QUT with a BFA (Acting) in 2006 and trained at HB Studio, New York in 2010. She was a facilitator for Playwriting Australia's Lotus (with Contemporary Asian Australian Performance) and Outreach programs, fostering emerging Australian writers, and is an advocate for diversity and inclusion in storytelling and in our industry. She is the Co-Artistic Director of Red Line Productions (at the Old Fitz). Catherine is a proud member of Actors' Equity.

ABOUT GRIFFIN

Griffin is the only theatre company in the country exclusively devoted to the development and staging of new Australian writing. Located in the historic SBW Stables Theatre, nestled in the heart of Kings Cross, Griffin has been Australia's home for the exploration of new stories since 1978.

We are the launch pad for new plays, ideas and writing that other theatres won't take a risk on. We boldly contribute to Australia's unique and powerful storytelling culture. Plays like *Prima Facie*, *Holding the Man* and *City of Gold* all had their world premieres at Griffin before going out to capture the national imagination. In the words of our longest-serving Artistic Director, **Ros Horin:**

"We are the theatre of first chances."

We are passionate about nurturing emerging and established practitioners alike. We pride ourselves on supporting our vast community of artists, audiences and supporters who consider our theatre their creative home. We help ambitious, bold, risk-taking and urgent Australian work get from the page onto the stage. We tell the stories that help us know who we are as a nation, and who we want to become.

Acknowledgement of Country

Griffin Theatre Company and the SBW Stables Theatre operate and tell stories on the unceded lands of the Gadigal of the Eora Nation. We acknowledge and honour Aboriginal and Torres Strait Islander people as the oldest continuous living culture on the planet, with more than 60,000 years of storytelling practice shaping and underpinning all aspects of Australian culture. It is a privilege that we do not take lightly: to work on this land, and to tell stories on its soil.

GRIFFIN THEATRE COMPANY
13 Craigend St
Kings Cross NSW 2011

02 9332 1052
info@griffintheatre.com.au
griffintheatre.com.au

SBW STABLES THEATRE
10 Nimrod St
Kings Cross NSW 2011

BOOKINGS
griffintheatre.com.au
02 9361 3817

GRIFFIN FAMILY

Patron
Seaborn, Broughton & Walford Foundation

Griffin acknowledges the generosity of the Seaborn, Broughton & Walford Foundation in allowing it the use of the SBW Stables Theatre rent free, less outgoings, since 1986.

Board
Bruce Meagher (Chair), Guillaume Babille, Simon Burke AO, Helen Dai, Lyndell Droga, Tim Duggan, Declan Greene, Julia Pincus, Lenore Robertson, Simone Whetton

Artistic Director & CEO
Declan Greene

Executive Director & CEO
Julieanne Campbell

Associate Artistic Director
Andrea James

Literary Manager (Acting)
Julian Larnach

Box Office Manager
Jackson Used

Ticketing Administrator
Nathan Harrison

Bar Manager
Alex Bryant-Smith

Front of House
Riordan Berry
Kandice Joy
Max Philips
Willo Young

Head of Development
Jake Shavikin

Relationships Manager
Ell Katte

Finance Manager
Kylie Richards

Finance Consultant
Emma Murphy

Marketing Manager (Acting)
Ang Collins

Marketing Coordinator
Sasha Meaney

Production Manager
Jeremy Page

Production Coordinator
Ally Moon

Senior Producer
Leila Enright

Programs Producer
Janine Lau

General Manager
Khym Scott

Ticketing & Administration Coordinator
Kate Marks

Strategic Insights Consultant
Peter O'Connell

Sustainability Coordinators
Ang Collins
Julian Larnach

Brand & Graphic Design
Alphabet

Web Developer
DevQuoll

Cover Photography
Brett Boardman

GRIFFIN DONORS

Income from Griffin activities covers less than 40% of our operating costs—leaving an ever-increasing gap for us to fill through government funding, sponsorship and the generosity of our individual supporters. Your support helps us bridge the gap and keep ticket prices affordable and our work at its best. To make a donation and a difference, contact Griffin on **9332 1052** or donate online at **griffintheatre.com.au**

PROGRAM PATRONS

Griffin Ambassadors
Robertson Foundation

Griffin Amplify
Girgensohn Foundation

Griffin Studio
Gil Appleton
Darin Cooper Foundation
Kiong Lee & Richard Funston
Rosemary Hannah & Lynette Preston
Ken & Lilian Horler
Malcolm Robertson Foundation
Geoff & Wendy Simpson OAM
Danielle Smith & Sean Carmody

Griffin Studio Workshop
Mary Ann Rolfe (Patron)
Iolanda Capodano & Juergen Krufczyk
Darin Cooper Foundation
Bob & Chris Ernst
Susan MacKinnon
Pip Rath & Wayne Lonergan
Walking up the Hill Foundation

Griffin Women's Initiative
Katrina Barter
Wendy Blacklock
Jessica Block
Christy Boyce & Madeleine Beaumont
Julieanne Campbell
Iolanda Capodanno
Laura Crennan

Jennifer Darin
Lyndell Droga
Judith Fox & Yvonne Stewart
Melinda Graham
Sherry Gregory
Rosemary Hannah & Lynette Preston
Antonia Haralambis
Ann Johnson
Roanne Knox
Tessa Leong
Tory Loudon
Susan MacKinnon
Julia Pincus
Ruth Ritchie
Lenore Robertson
Deanne Weir
Simone Whetton

PRODUCTION PARTNERS 2023

***Jailbaby* by Suzie Miller**
Andrew Post & Sue Quill

PRODUCTION PARTNERS 2022

***Whitefella Yella Tree* by Dylan Van Den Berg**
Lisa Barker & Don Russell
Darin Cooper Foundation
Robert Dick & Erin Shiel
Lyndell & Daniel Droga
Danny Gilbert AM & Kathleen Gilbert
Rosemary Hannah & Lynette Preston
Bruce Meagher & Greg Waters
Richard McHugh & Kate Morgan
Julia Pincus & Ian Learmonth
Pip Rath & Wayne Lonergan

SEASON DONORS

Company Patron $100,000+
Neilson Foundation

Season Patron $50,000+
Girgensohn Foundation
Robertson Foundation

Mainstage Donors $20,000+
Anonymous (1)
Darin Cooper Foundation
Robert Dick & Erin Shiel
Rosemary Hannah & Lynette Preston
Julia Pincus & Ian Learmonth
Mary Ann Rolfe

Production Donors $10,000+
Lisa Barker & Don Russell
Gordon & Marie Esden
Abraham & Helen James
Ingrid Kaiser
Nathan Mayfield
Richard McHugh & Kate Morgan
Bruce Meagher & Greg Waters
Tim Minchin
Peter & Dianne O'Connell
Pip Rath & Wayne Lonergan
The WeirAnderson Foundation

Rehearsal Donors $5,000–$9,999
Anonymous (1)
Antoinette Albert
Gil Appleton
Wendy Blacklock
Ellen Borda
Susan Carleton
Bernard Coles

Ian Dickson
Lyndell & Daniel Droga
Danny Gilbert AM & Kathleen Gilbert
Libby Higgin
Ken & Lilian Horler
Lambert Bridge Foundation
Kiong Lee & Richard Funston
Lee Lewis & Brett Boardman
Rosemary Lucas & Robert Yuen
Sophie McCarthy & Antony Green
Catriona Morgan-Hunn
Anthony Paull
Rebel Penfold-Russell OAM
Geoff & Wendy Simpson OAM
The Sky Foundation
Merilyn Sleigh & Raoul de Ferranti
Danielle Smith & Sean Carmody
Walking Up the Hill Foundation

Final Draft Donors
$3,000–$4,999

Corinne & Bryan
Bob & Chris Ernst
Jocelyn Goyen
Sherry Gregory
James Hartwright & Kerrin D'Arcy
Roanne & John Knox
Susan MacKinnon
Don & Leslie Parsonage
Leslie Stern

Workshop Donors
$1,000–$2,999

Anonymous (6)
Baly Douglass Foundation
Katrina Barter
Helen Bauer & Helen Lynch AM
Cherry & Peter Best
Jessica Block
Christy Boyce & Madeleine Beaumont
Dr Bernadette Brennan

Anne Britton
Stephen & Annabelle Burley
Iolanda Capodano & Juergen Krufczyk
Julieanne Campbell
Louise Christie
Anna Cleary
Bryony & Tim Cox
Sally Crawford
Laura Crennan
Cris Croker & David West
Ros & Paul Espie
Brian Everingham
Jan Ewert
John & Libby Fairfax
Sandra Forbes
Jennifer Giles
Nicky Gluyas
Melinda Graham
Peter Gray & Helen Thwaites
Antonia Haralambis
Kate Harrison
John Head
Mark Hopkinson & Michelle Opie
Michael Jackson
Ann Johnson
David & Adrienne Kitching
Elizabeth Laverty
Benjamin Law
Tessa Leong
Richard & Elizabeth Longes
Tory Loudon
Kyrsty Macdonald & Christopher Hazell
Prudence Manrique
Lorin Muhlmann
Ian Neuss & Penny Young
David Nguyen
Shaan Perera
Ian Phipps
Martin Portus
Annabel Ritchie
In memory of Katherine Robertson
Sylvia Rosenblum
Jann Skinner
Ann & Quinn Sloan
Stuart Thomas
Elizabeth Thompson

Mike Thompson
Sue Thomson
Janet Wahlquist
Richard Weinstein & Richard Benedict
Simone Whetton
Rob White & Lisa Hamilton
Rosemary White
Paul & Jennifer Winch
Elizabeth Wing

Reading Donors
$500–$999

Anonymous (3)
Brian Abel
Priscilla Adey
Jane Albert
Amity Alexander
Wendy Ashton
Robyn Ayres
Melissa Ball
Phillip Black
Claire Bornhoffen
Larry Boyd & Barbara Caine AM
Tim Capelin
Jane Christensen
Michael Diamond AM MBE
Max Dingle OAM
Elizabeth Diprose
David Earp
Leonie Flannery
Alan Froude & David Round
Peter Graves
Erica Gray
Stephanie & Andrew Harrison
David Hoskins & Paul McKnight
Sylvia Hrovatin
Nicki Jam
Mira Joksovic
Matt Jones & Rebecca Bourne Jones
Colleen Mary Kane
Susan J Kath
Patricia Lynch
Ian & Elizabeth MacDonald
Suzanne & Anthony Maple-Brown
Robert Marks

Nick Read
Chris Marrable & Kate Richardson
Simon Marrable & Anna Kasper
Christopher Matthies
Christopher McCabe
John McCallum & Jenny Nicholls
Daniela McMurdo
Jacqui Mercer
John Mitchell
Neville Mitchell
Keith Moynihan
Patricia Novikoff
Carolyn Penfold
Belinda Piggott & David Ojerholm
Virginia Pursell
Alex-Oonagh Redmond
Bill Harris
Gemma Rygate
Rob & Rae Spence
Mary Stollery & Eric Dole
Catherine Sullivan & Alexandra Bowen
Ariadne Vromen
Robyn Fortescue & Rosie Wagstaff
Helen Wicker

First Draft Donors $200-$499

Anonymous (11)
Susan Ambler
Elizabeth Antonievich
William Armitage
Chris Baker
Jan Barr
John Bell AO, OBE
Edwina Birch
Andrew Bowmer
Peter Brown
Wendy Buswell
Ruth Campbell
David Caulfield
Amanda Clark
Sue Clark
Louise Costanzo
Brendan Crotty & Darryl Toohey

Bryan Cutler
Sue Donnelly
Peter Duerden
Anna Duggan
Kathy Esson
Elizabeth Evatt
Michael Eyers
Helen Ford
Judith Fox
Eva Gerber
Jock Given
Deane Golding
Keith Gow
Virginia & Kieran Greene
Jo Grisard
Edwina Guinness
Ruth Guss
Kate Haddock
Raewyn Harlock
Robert Henderson & Marijke Conrade
Grania Hickley
Matthew Huxtable
Marian & Nabeel Ibrahim
Andrew Inglis
James Landon-Smith
Penelope Latey
Liz Locke
Danielle Long
Norman Long
Noella Lopez
Maruschka Loupis
Anni MacDougall
Claire McCaughan
Louise McDonald
Duncan McKay
Paula McLean
Stephen McNamara
Anne Miehs
Julia Mitchell
Mark Mitchell
Sarah Mort
Margaret Murphy
Carolyn Newman
Suzanne Osmond
Catherine & Joshua Palmer
Peter Pezzutti
Christopher Powell
Janelle Prescott
Andrew Pringle

Dorothy & Adit Rao
Tracey Robson
Ann Rocca
Catherine Rothery
Kevin & Shirley Ryan
Dimity Scales
Julia Selby
Natalie Shea
Vivienne Skinner
Bridget Smith
Vanda & Martin Smith
Yvonne Stewart
Augusta Supple
Danny Tomic
Rachel Trigg
Samantha Turley
Adam Van Rooijen
Julie Whitfield
Eve Wynhausen
Robert Yuen
William Zappa

We would also like to thank Peter O'Connell for his expertise, guidance and time.

CURRENT AS OF 18 JANUARY 2023

GRIFFIN SPONSORS

Griffin would like to thank the following:

OUR PARTNERS

Government Supporters

Benefactor

Creative Partners

alphabet.   GIRGENSOHN FOUNDATION

Company Sponsors

  SATURDAY PAPER

Griffin Theatre Company is assisted by the Australian Government through the Australia Council, its arts funding and advisory body; and the NSW Government through Create NSW.

www.currency.com.au

Visit Currency Press' website now to:

- Order books
- Browse through our full list of titles including plays, screenplays, theory and reference/criticism, performance handbooks, educational texts and more
- Choose a play for your school or performance group by cast specs
- Seek performance rights
- Find out about performing arts news and sign up for our newsletter
- For students: read our study guides
- For teachers: access free curriculum information and teacher notes

We are also on Facebook and Instagram (@currencypress). Join the conversation!

The performing arts publisher